FIE

C000071913

MICROSOFT
ACCESS 2

PUBLISHED BY

Microsoft Press
A Division of Microsoft Corporation
One Microsoft Way
Redmond, Washington 98052-6399

Copyright © 1994 by Stephen L. Nelson, Inc.

Library of Congress Cataloging-in-Publication Data
Nelson, Stephen L., 1959-
    Field guide to Microsoft Access 2 /Stephen L. Nelson.
        p.   cm.
    Includes index.
    ISBN 1-55615-581-6
    1. Database management. 2. Microsoft Access
    I. Title.
QA76.9.D3N45   1994
005.75'65--dc20   94-7668
                                                CIP

Printed and bound in the United States of America.

    4 5 6 7 8 9 QBP 9 8 7 6 5

Distributed to the book trade in Canada by Macmillan
of Canada, a division of Canada Publishing Corporation.

A CIP catalogue record for this book is available from
the British Library.

Microsoft Press books are available through
booksellers and distributors worldwide. For further
information about international editions, contact your
local Microsoft Corporation office. Or contact Microsoft
Press International directly at fax (206) 936-7329.

Acquisitions Editor: Lucinda Rowley
Project Editor: Tara Powers-Hausmann
Technical Contact: Mary DeJong

FIELD GUIDE TO

MICROSOFT ACCESS 2

Stephen L. Nelson

The Field Guide to Microsoft Access is divided into four sections. These sections are designed to help you find the information you need quickly.

1 ENVIRONMENT

Terms and ideas you'll want to know to get the most out of Access. All the basic parts of Access are shown and explained. The emphasis here is on quick answers, but most topics are cross-referenced so you can find out more if you want to.

Diagrams of key windows components, with quick definitions, cross-referenced to more complete information.

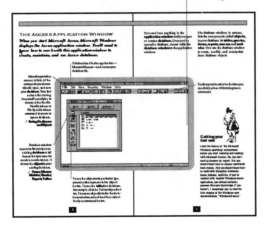

Tipmeister

Watch for me as you use this Field Guide. I'll point out helpful hints and let you know what to watch for.

15 ACCESS A TO Z

An alphabetic list of commands, tasks, terms, and procedures.

Definitions of key concepts and terms, and examples showing you why you should know them.

Quick identification of icons and groups.

Step-by-step guides to performing most Access tasks.

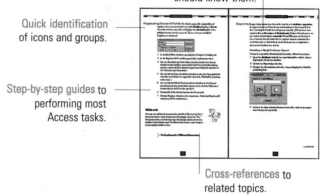

Cross-references to related topics.

127 TROUBLESHOOTING

A guide to common problems—how to avoid them and what to do when they occur.

145 QUICK REFERENCE

Useful indexes, including a full list of menu commands, shortcut keys, and more.

157 INDEX

Complete reference to all elements of the Field Guide.

INTRODUCTION

In the field and on expedition, you need practical solutions. Fast. This Field Guide provides just these sorts of lightning quick answers. But take two minutes and read the Introduction. It explains how this unusual little book works.

HOW TO USE THIS BOOK

Sometime during grade school, my parents gave me a field guide to North American birds. With its visual approach, its maps, and its numerous illustrations, that guide delivered hours of enjoyment. The book also helped me better understand and more fully appreciate the birds in my neighborhood. And the small book fit neatly in a child's rucksack. But I'm getting off the track.

WHAT IS A FIELD GUIDE?

This book works in the same way as that field guide. It organizes information visually with numerous illustrations. And it does this in a way that helps you more easily understand and, yes, even enjoy working with Microsoft Access. For new users, the Field Guide provides a visual path to the essential information necessary to start using Microsoft Access. But the Field Guide isn't only for beginners. For experienced users, it provides concise, easy-to-find descriptions of Microsoft Access tasks, terms, and techniques.

WHEN YOU HAVE A QUESTION

Let me explain then how to find the information you need. You'll usually want to begin with the first section, Environment, which is really a visual index. You find the picture that shows what you want to do or the task you have a question about. If you want to know how to store information in a **table,** for example, you flip to pp. 6-7, which show a table.

Next you read the captions that describe the parts of the picture—or key elements of Microsoft Access. Say, for example, that you're new to the business of creating databases and want to become familiar with database terms such as **rows** and **columns.** The window on pp. 6-7 includes captions that describe the parts of a table—including its rows and columns. These key elements appear in **boldface** type to make them stand out.

WHEN YOU NEED MORE INFORMATION

You'll notice that some captions are followed by a little paw print and additional **boldface** terms. These refer to entries in the second section, Access A to Z, and provide more information related to the caption's contents. (The paw print shows you how to track down the information you need. Get it?)

Access A to Z is a dictionary of more than 100 entries that define terms and describe tasks. (After you've worked with Microsoft Access a bit or if you're already an experienced user, you'll often be able to turn directly to this section.) So, if you have just read the caption that says tables can be joined with common fields, you can flip to the **Joining Tables** entry in Access A to Z.

Any time an entry in Access A to Z appears as a term within an entry, I'll **boldface** it the first time it appears in the entry. For example, as part of describing what a Microsoft Access database is, I tell you that a database includes **query** objects. In this case, the word **query** will appear in bold letters—alerting you to the presence of a Query entry. If you don't understand the term or want to do a bit of brushing up, you can flip to the entry for more information.

WHEN YOU HAVE A PROBLEM

The third section, Troubleshooting, describes problems that new or casual users of Microsoft Access often encounter. Following each problem description, I list one or more solutions you can employ to fix the problem.

WHEN YOU WONDER ABOUT A COMMAND

The Quick Reference describes the menu commands that appear on the startup application window (which is the window that shows before you open or create a database) and the menu commands that appear immediately after you open or create a database. If you want to know what a specific command does, turn to the Quick Reference. Don't forget about the Index either. You can look there to find all references in this book to any single topic.

CONVENTIONS USED HERE

I have developed some conventions to make using this book easier for you. Rather than use wordy phrases, such as "Activate the File menu and then choose the Print command," to describe how you choose a command, I'm just going to say, "Choose the File Print command."

When some technique requires you to click a toolbar button, I'm going to tell you to select the tool. (I'll show a picture of the tool in the margin, so you won't have any trouble identifying it.)

ENVIRONMENT

Need to get the lay of the land quickly? Then the Environment is the place to start. It defines the key terms you'll need to know and the core ideas you should understand as you begin exploring Microsoft Access.

WHAT IS A DATABASE?

A database is a collection of related information.

In a paper-based database, you might store information all over the place—for example, in filing cabinet drawers or even on top of your desk. This makes using the information and keeping it up to date difficult.

❖ Databases

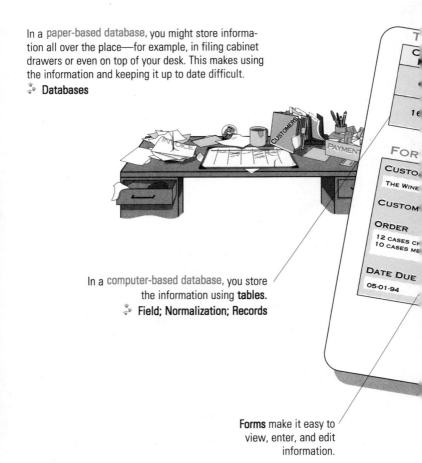

In a computer-based database, you store the information using **tables**.

❖ Field; Normalization; Records

Forms make it easy to view, enter, and edit information.

Database managers, such as Microsoft Access, provide tools that let you store database information. They also provide tools that make it easier to use and update the information in a database. ❖ **Forms; Query; Reports**

Queries easily gather database information according to criteria you specify.

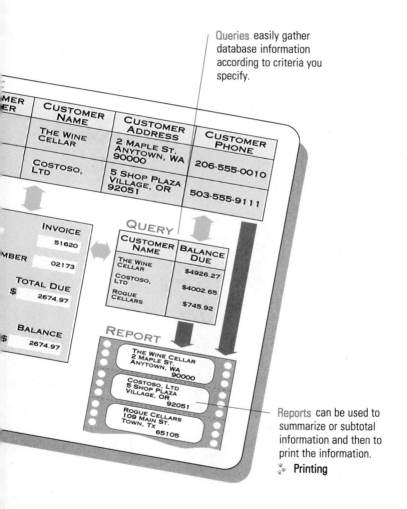

MER ER	CUSTOMER NAME	CUSTOMER ADDRESS	CUSTOMER PHONE
	THE WINE CELLAR	2 MAPLE ST. ANYTOWN, WA 90000	206-555-0010
	COSTOSO, LTD	5 SHOP PLAZA VILLAGE, OR 92051	503-555-9111

INVOICE
51620

MBER
02173

TOTAL DUE
$ 2674.97

BALANCE
$ 2674.97

QUERY

CUSTOMER NAME	BALANCE DUE
THE WINE CELLAR	$4926.27
COSTOSO, LTD	$4002.65
ROGUE CELLARS	$745.92

REPORT

THE WINE CELLAR
2 MAPLE ST.
ANYTOWN, WA 90000

COSTOSO, LTD
5 SHOP PLAZA
VILLAGE, OR 92051

ROGUE CELLARS
109 MAIN ST.
TOWN, TX 65105

Reports can be used to summarize or subtotal information and then to print the information.
❖ **Printing**

3

THE ACCESS APPLICATION WINDOW

When you start Microsoft Access, Microsoft Windows displays the Access application window. You'll need to know how to work with this application window to create, maintain, and use Access databases.

Title bar identifies the application—Microsoft Access—and names your database file.

Menu bar provides menus, or lists, of the commands you choose to build, open, and save your **database**. Your first action after starting Access will usually be to choose either the File New Database or File Open Database command to create or open a database.
 ⁖ **Saving Databases and Objects**

Database window appears after you open an existing **database** or tell Access that you want to create a new database. It shows the **objects** in your existing database.
 ⁖ **Forms; Macros; Modules; Queries; Reports; Tables**

Microsoft Acc

File **Edit** **View** **Security** **Window** **Help**

Database: CUSTOMER

New   **Open**   **Design**

Table   **Tables**
Query   Customers
Form   Order Details
Report   Orders
Macro   Products
Module   Projects

Ready

To see the objects of a particular type, you select the representative object button. To see the **tables** in a database, for example, click the Tables object button. To use an object listed in the database window, select it and then select the Open command button.

You won't see anything in the **application window** until you open or create a **database.** Once you've opened a database, Access adds the **database window** to the application window.

The database window, in essence, lists the components, called **objects,** in your database: its **tables, queries, forms, reports, macros**, and **modules.** You use the database window to create, modify, and manipulate these database objects.

Toolbar provides shortcut buttons you can click in place of choosing menu commands.

Getting your feet wet

Learn the basics of the Microsoft Windows operating environment before you start learning and working with Microsoft Access. No, you don't need to become an expert. But you should know how to choose commands from menus. And you should know how to work with dialog box elements: boxes, buttons, and lists. If you've worked with another Windows-based application, you almost certainly possess this core knowledge. If you haven't, I encourage you to read the first chapter of the Windows user documentation, "Windows Basics."

WORKING WITH TABLES

In a relational database, you store the information you collect in tables.

Tables organize database information into columns and rows. An Access database usually includes at least one table, but it can include many tables. You create tables by clicking the Table object button and then the New command button.

❧ Importing Data; Normalization

Microsoft Access

File Edit View Format Records Window Help

Table: Customers

CustomerID	FirstName	LastName	Address	City
1	Patty	Simmons	512 Wetmore	Pine Lake
2	Ralph	Walters	234 Garden Court	Seattle
3	Meg	Mozart	9200 Squire Ave	Tacoma
4	Susan	Hughes	661 Fort Casey	Whidbey
5	Sherlock	Wriston	22B Baker St.	George
6	James	Donald	914 Freemont St.	Ellensbur
7	Patty	Simmons	512 Wetmore	Pine Lake
8	Ralph	Walters	234 Garden Court	Seattle
9	Meg	Mozart	9200 Squire Ave	Tacoma
10	Susan	Hughes	661 Fort Casey	Whidbey
11	Sherlock			
12	James			
(Counter)				

Record: 12

Datasheet View

ProjectID	ProjectName
1	Simmons Kitchen
2	Simmons Roof
3	Walters Floors
4	Walters Roof
5	Mozart Bath
6	Hughes Roof
7	Hughes Kitchen
8	Wriston sunroom
9	Wriston hottub
10	Wriston Roof
11	Donald Gazebo
12	Donald Deck
(Counter)	

Record: 4 of 12

Rows segregate your table entries, or **records**. In a database that stores information about customers, for example, you might have a table that lists customer addresses. In such a **table**, each customer address would go into its own table row.

Datasheets, such as the one shown here, let you view the records in a table. You can directly edit the information in a table by editing the cells in a datasheet. It's usually easier, however, to use a form.

❧ Query; Reports; Views

6

Database creation begins with the description of the table or tables you'll use to store the database's information. You create a table by describing the columns, or fields, that the table uses to store information.

After you describe the table's columns, you begin entering data into the table, one row, or record, at a time. You can enter data directly into a table using datasheets or indirectly into a table using a form.

PhoneNumber
555-1234
555-1235
555-4325
555-3456
555-0098
555-0031
555-1734
555-9235
555-4325
555-3456
555-0098

Columns organize the records in your table into **fields**. In a database that stores information about customers, for example, all the customer names might go into a single column. In describing a table column you also describe the type of data that can be stored in the column—text, numbers, and so on.

💠 **Data Types; Field Properties; Validation Rules**

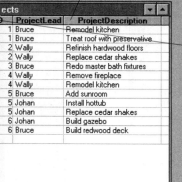

ects		
	ProjectLead	ProjectDescription
1	Bruce	Remodel kitchen
1	Bruce	Treat roof with preservative
2	Wally	Refinish hardwood floors
2	Wally	Replace cedar shakes
3	Bruce	Redo master bath fixtures
4	Wally	Remove fireplace
4	Wally	Remodel kitchen
5	Bruce	Add sunroom
5	Johan	Install hottub
5	Johan	Replace cedar shakes
6	Johan	Build gazebo
6	Bruce	Build redwood deck

Common fields let you combine, or join, tables. In a two-table customer database, for example, you might create and use a customer number field in both tables so that they can be combined in a **query** and for **forms** and **reports**.

💠 **Common Fields; Index; Joining Tables; Primary Key; Referential Integrity; Relationships**

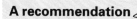

A recommendation

Sketch out which tables your database will need and which fields should go into each table before you start creating tables. You'll save yourself time in the long run by doing so.

WORKING WITH FORMS

Once you describe the tables in a database, you can enter records into the tables using a Microsoft Access form.

Entering a record with a form simply requires that you fill in each of the text boxes.

Editing a record requires that you first display the **record** and then make the changes using the text boxes. Use these buttons to move backward and forward through a table's or a query's records.

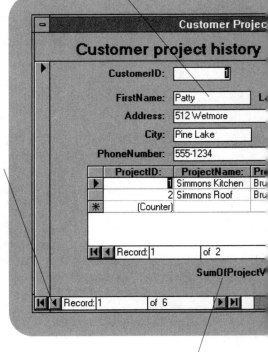

Forms you create from scratch can use any element of the Windows user interface.

✦ Control Wizard; Macro Button

An Access form, which is another type of database object, lets you enter, view, and print information from a table or a query. You can create simple forms quickly using the Form Wizard. You simply tell Access that you want to create a new form and identify the table or tables you want to fill or view. (You can also create forms from scratch.)

Although forms will often be used to enter data into tables, they aren't limited to data entry and data editing. You can also use them to view the data in a table or a query.

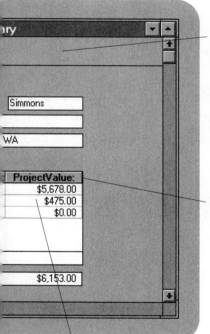

Main/Subforms let you view or enter one record from one **table** or **query** and all the related **records** from another table or query. Access lets you create other types of forms, including those that let you view or enter one record at a time, those that display records from more than one table, and those that display **graphs**.

☙ Forms; Macro Buttons

The Subform show the records related to the Main form record.

Calculation fields show the result of some calculation **expression**. You don't need to enter calculated values. Access calculates them for you.

☙ Functions; Mathematical Operators

WORKING WITH QUERIES

A query is a question you ask about data in your database. "Who are my customers?" is a query, for example.

Dynasets display the results of a **query.** A dynaset then is the answer to your question. This dynaset would answer the question, "What is the total value of the projects I've performed for each of my customers?"

Joining tables during a **query** makes it possible to combine tables. To combine tables, the tables must use a **common field.**
⁘ Equi-join; Outer-join; Primary Table; Relationship

Sort orders, which you specify as part of describing the **query,** determine how query results are organized.
⁘ Index; Primary Key

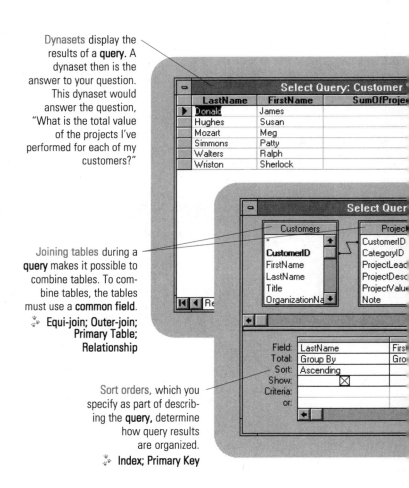

To ask the question, you describe the **query** in precise detail by creating a query object.

You can ask Microsoft Access to summarize, organize, and even update database information as it answers your question. For example, you can tell Access to count the number of customers in a customers **table.** You can tell Access to total the amounts customers owe. And you can tell Access to calculate a finance charge and add this charge to the amount a customer owes you.

:* **Action Query; QBE; Query**

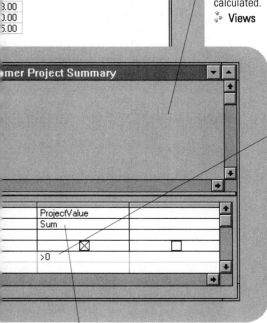

Design view of a query object describes the question that **query** asks in precise detail, including any selection criteria, sort orders, or totals you want calculated.

:* **Views**

Selection criteria are often essential to answering the **query** because they determine which records appear in the **dynaset.** This selection criteria tells Access that you only want to see project value information for customers with project values greater than zero.

:* **Filter; Logical Operators; QBE**

Subtotals can be easily added to a **query** by telling Microsoft Access how it should group and summarize query results.

PRINTING DATABASE INFORMATION

You can print information from or about any of the objects in a database. You can, for example, print a table to show its contents or print a query's dynaset to show the answer to the question the query asks.

Reports are another type of database **object**. You can create them using a Wizard. You display an on-screen version of the report by opening the report object. When you do, Microsoft Access displays the print preview window that shows how the report's pages look.

Print the report by choosing the File Print command or the Print tool. You can also print a table's **datasheet** or a query **dynaset** by choosing the File Print command or the Print tool.

.•. Printing; Reports

Projects by customers

03-Mar-94

ProjectLead   ProjectDescr

FullName

Build
Bruce   Buil
Johan

Donald, James

Wally
Wally

Hughes, Susan

Bru

Mozart, Meg

Simmons, Patty

Walters, Ralph

Although you can print the information shown in a table or a query simply by choosing the File Print command, you can also create **reports,** another type of database **object,** to organize, summarize, and format the information in a single table or a single query.

The easiest way to create a report is by using the Report Wizards. The Report Wizards create several common reports for you by stepping you through a series of dialog boxes that ask about the information you want to see and about how the information should be organized.

☞ **Mailing Labels**

jectValue

$2,275.00

$3,200.00

$5,475.00

7.02%

$22,765.00

$5,400.00

$28,165.00

36.10%

master bath fixtures

$4,000.00

$4,000.00

5.13%

$475.00

Treat roof with preservative

Remodel kitchen

$5,678.00

$6,153.00

7.89%

$7,800.00

Replace cedar shakes

Printing object design information

You can print information about the design of a database object by opening the database object in a design view and then choosing the File Print Definition command.

Report data comes from either a database **table** or a **query.** You identify which table or query supplies the data as part of creating the report object.

ACCESS
A TO Z

Maybe it's not a jungle out there. But you'll still want to keep a survival kit close at hand. Access A to Z, which starts on the next page, is just such a survival kit. It lists in alphabetic order the tools, terms, and techniques you'll need to know.

Access Basic Access Basic is the programming language that is
built in to Microsoft Access. Access Basic is way cool. It's
also way beyond the scope of this little book. For information about Access Basic, see your Microsoft Access
user documentation.

Macros; Modules

Action Query An action query is a **query** that changes or deletes
data in the queried **tables**—for example, a query that calculates customer finance charges and adds these amounts
to the customer balances. Microsoft Access provides four
types of action queries: update, append, delete, and make
table. I'll briefly describe how each works in the para-
graphs that follow.

Creating and Running Update Action Queries

An update action query changes table **records**. To create an update
query, you go about business as usual until you're sure the **select**
query works the way it should. Then you choose the Query Update
command while in design view.

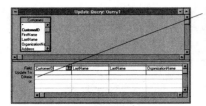

Access, sensing that
something big is about to
happen, changes the
object window name to
Update Query and adds a
new row entitled Update
To.

You enter the value or the text (or the **expression** that returns the
value or the text) into the appropriate Update To cells. Then you run
the query in the usual way.

Two friendly suggestions regarding update queries

Let me throw out a couple of suggestions if you haven't done an update query before: (1) Run some tests on sample data to make sure your update query works the way it's supposed to; (2) back up your database before you run the update query just in case something bad happens or if you ignored my first suggestion.

Creating and Running Append Action Queries

You can add, or append, the query results shown in a **dynaset** to an existing table. To do this, follow these steps:

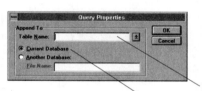

1 Create and run the select query that produces a dynaset with the records you want to add.

2 Choose the Query Append command. Microsoft Access displays the Query Properties dialog box.

3 Identify the table to which records should be added.

4 Identify the database in which the table is an object.

5 Choose OK to close the Query Properties dialog box.

 6 Choose the Query Run command or select the Run tool.

continues

Action Query *(continued)*

Creating and Running Delete Action Queries

You can delete the query results shown in a dynaset from the queried tables. But before you run a delete query, you should **back up** your data. Once you've backed up your data, follow these steps to run your delete query:

1 Create and run the select query that produces a dynaset with the records you want to delete.

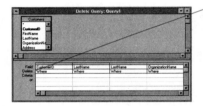

2 Choose the Query Delete command. Microsoft Access adds a Delete Row to the **QBE** grid and changes the object window title bar to Delete Query.

3 Choose the Query Run command or select the Run tool.

A

Creating and Running Make Table Action Queries

You can add the query results shown in a dynaset to a new table. To do this, follow these steps:

1 Create and run the select query that produces a dynaset with the records you want to add.

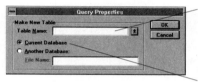

2 Choose the Query Make Table command. Access displays the Query Properties dialog box.

3 Identify the new table to which the records should be added.

4 Identify the database in which the new table should be an object.

5 Choose OK to close the Query Properties dialog box.

 6 Choose the Query Run command or select the Run tool.

continues

Action Query *(continued)*

Saving an Action Query

You can save an action query in the same manner you save a regular old select query. When you close the query object window, for example, Access will ask if you want to save the query. If you answer in the affirmative and provide a query name, Microsoft Access adds the query as an object to your database.

Because action queries change data, Microsoft Access sticks an exclamation point in front of the query object name on the **Database window**. Remember: Opening one of these action queries may change your data!

Active and Inactive Windows
The active **document window** is the one you see in the **application window**. Any commands you choose affect the **document** in the active document window.

The active application window—such as the Microsoft Access application window—is the one that appears in front of any other application windows on your screen. (Cleverly, this is called the foreground. The inactive application windows, if there are inactive applications, appear in the background.)

Activating Application Windows

You can activate a different application window by clicking the window or by choosing the Switch To command from the Control menu.

Activating Document Windows

You can activate a different document window by clicking the window or by choosing the Window menu command that names the window.

ANSI Characters

The ANSI character set includes all the ASCII characters your keyboard shows plus the special characters your keyboard doesn't show, such as the Japanese yen symbol (¥) or the British pound symbol (£). Even though these special characters don't appear on your keyboard, you can still use them in **fields** as long as you know the ANSI character code. (You can get ANSI character codes from the Windows user documentation.)

Adding ANSI Characters

To enter an ANSI character, position the insertion point where you want the character, hold down the Alt key, and then, using the numeric keypad, enter the ANSI code for that character. For example, the ANSI character code for the Japanese yen symbol is 0165. To enter a yen symbol into a document, hold down Alt and type *0165* using the numeric keypad. (Be sure to include the zero and turn on your Num Lock key.)

Application

Applications are the programs you buy down at the software store or through the mail to do work—work like word processing, spreadsheeting, database stuff, accounting, and a bunch of other tasks as well.

Microsoft sells several well-known and very popular applications including Microsoft Access (the database program this book describes), Microsoft Excel (a spreadsheet program), and Microsoft Word (a word processor). There are lots of other popular and well-known applications too: WordPerfect, Lotus 1-2-3, and Quicken are the names of just three.

Application Errors Sometimes an **application**—it could be Access or another application—asks Windows to do the impossible. When this happens, Windows displays a message box that alerts you to an application error.

⁙ **Troubleshooting: You Get an Application Error**

Application Window The application window is the rectangle in which an **application** such as Microsoft Access displays its menu bar, toolbars, and any open **document windows**.

ASCII Text Files An ASCII text file is simply a file that uses only ASCII characters. You can import an ASCII text file into database applications such as Access using the File Import command.

Sharing data among applications

A last resort method for sharing data among applications is to create an ASCII text file. This works because many applications—spreadsheets, databases, and accounting programs among others—produce text files.

⁙ **Importing Data**

AutoForm Wizard The AutoForm Wizard will build a **form** for you automatically. All you need to do is display the table or the query datasheet for which you want to create a form and then select the AutoForm tool.

C

AutoReport Wizard

 The AutoReport Wizard will build a report for you automatically. All you need to do is display the table or query datasheet for which you want to create a report and then select the AutoReport tool.

Back Up

The easiest way to back up database files is to copy them to a floppy disk. If you want to make things slightly easier and you've got a handful of files, you may also be able to use the Backup utility if you're running MS-DOS version 6 or later. This isn't a book about MS-DOS, so I won't describe here how the Backup command works. You'll need to refer to the MS-DOS user documentation.

I need to point out here, however, that if you've got a lot of stuff to back up—like a 50-megabyte database file, say—you'll want to back up to a tape. And for that you'll need to use a third-party Windows backup utility or an MS-DOS backup utility. Oh. One more thing: Microsoft Access database files use the file extension MDB.

Calculated Controls

Calculated controls are **control objects** that calculate expressions. They sometimes appear on **forms**, and they always appear on **reports** that summarize.

C

Calculated Fields

You can add a calculated field to a query and to a form.

Calculating a Value for a Query

To calculate a value for a query, follow these steps:

1 Select the column of the query design window into which the calculated field should be placed.

2 Enter the calculated field name followed by a colon.

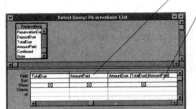

3 Enter a formula that describes the calculation. This calculated field computes the remaining amount due by subtracting the AmountPaid field from the TotalDue field. You can use field names (but not calculated field names) as long as you include them in brackets ([ ]). You can use any of the Access mathematical operators. You can use values. You can also use functions.

Concatenating Text

You can concatenate, or combine, separate fields in a query by using the & (concatenation) operator. For example, if you've stored a person's last and first names in two separate fields, you can combine them with a space by using this expression: Name:[First Name]&" "&[Last Name].

Limiting the Records Used in a Calculation

You can limit, or restrict, which records' fields are used in a calculation by using the Where summary operator. To do this, enter the operator Where into the TotalDue row of the QBE grid. Then enter the criteria that selects the records you want to include.

Clipboard Ever see the television show "Star Trek"? If you did, you may remember the transporter room. It let the Starship Enterprise move Captain Kirk, Mr. Spock, and just about anything else just about anywhere. The Clipboard is the Microsoft Windows equivalent of the Enterprise's transporter room. With the Clipboard, Windows and Windows-based applications, such as Microsoft Access, easily move just about anything anywhere. When working with a Windows-based application, you can use the Clipboard to move chunks of text, tables, and even graphic images to and from different files. You can also use the Clipboard to move text, **tables,** and graphic images between Windows applications, such as from Microsoft Paintbrush to Microsoft Access.

To move information around via the Clipboard, you actually use the Edit menu's Cut, Copy, and Paste commands. So you don't have to know all that much about the Clipboard to make good use of it. One thing you should remember about the Clipboard, however, is that it stores what you've copied or cut temporarily. After you copy or cut, the next time you do so, the previous Clipboard contents are replaced. And when you exit Windows, the Clipboard contents are erased.

Closing Database Objects You close database objects so that they don't consume memory, so that they don't clutter your screen, and so that they don't just plain annoy you.

Closing a Single Database Object

To close a single object, either double-click its Control-menu box, or be sure the object is visible and then choose the File Close command.

If there are unsaved changes

Access won't close an object to which you have made design changes but not yet saved. It will first ask if you want to save your design changes. If you say, "Well, yeah, that seems like a good idea," the application then saves the modified object definition.

Closing Databases You close a database file by exiting Access or by opening a new database file. (You can have only one database file open so Access closes the first database file before it opens the next database file.) You don't need to save changes to the data in the database file. Access does that automatically.

⁂ **Exiting Microsoft Access; Database**

Common Fields Common fields are the **fields** that **tables** in a database share. If your database is correctly designed, you probably use common fields to connect, or join, tables. (If a common field isn't being used to join tables, it may indicate a data redundancy.)

Common field names and properties

It's a good idea to use the same name for common fields. Identical names make it super-easy for Access to join the tables. Common fields should use the same field properties in each table in which they appear, with one exception: If you use a Counter field in one table, the same field in the other table should be a Number with the Long format if the two tables have a one-to-many relationship.

 Field Property

Control-menu Commands
Control-menu commands appear, not surprisingly, on the Control menus of application windows, object windows, and dialog boxes.

To activate the Control menu of a window or a dialog box, you click the Control-menu box. (It's the little hyphen-in-a-box in the upper left corner of the window or the dialog box.)

Control-menu commands let you manipulate the window or the dialog box in the following ways.

Restore

This command undoes the last minimize or maximize command. Handy if you're fooling around with the Control menu and you make a terrible mistake.

Move

This command tells Windows you want to move the window or the dialog box. Windows, ever mindful of your feelings, changes the mouse pointer to a four-headed arrow. Once this happens, use the Up and Down direction keys to change the screen position of the window or the dialog box.

continues

Control-menu Commands *(continued)*

Size

This command tells Windows you want to change the size of the
window. When you choose this command, Windows changes the
mouse pointer to a four-headed arrow. You change the window size
by using the Up and Down direction keys to move the bottom border
and by using the Left and Right direction keys to move the right
border.

Minimize

This command tells Windows in no uncertain terms that it should
remove the window from the screen. Windows follows your
command, but to remind you of the minimized window, it displays a
tiny picture, called an icon. Because you can't see the Control menu of
a minimized window, simply click a minimized window icon to display
its Control menu.

Maximize

This command tells Windows that it should make the window or the
dialog box as big as it can. If you maximize an application window—
such as the Microsoft Access window—Windows makes the
application window as big as your monitor.

Close

This command removes the window or the dialog box from the
monitor. There's more to this command than first meets the eye,
however. If you close an application window, you actually close the
application. If you close an object window, you also close the object
displayed in the object window. If you made design changes to the
object that haven't yet been saved, Microsoft Access will ask if you
want to do this before it closes the object. Closing a dialog box is the
same as choosing Cancel.

Next

This command—wait a minute. You can guess, right? This command displays the next object window in a stack of object windows.

Switch To

Cool. A power-user tool. This command appears only on the Control menus of application windows. It tells Windows that you want to see the Task List—presumably so that you can start another application or so that you can move another application you've previously started to the foreground.

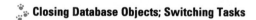

About the Control-menu commands

You won't always see all these commands on a Control menu. Windows displays only those that make sense in the current situation.

❖ **Closing Database Objects; Switching Tasks**

Control Objects Controls objects are the objects you see on a **form,** a **report,** or a **graph.** On a form, for example, the boxes and buttons that appear on the form as well as any labels that describe the form and its boxes and buttons are control objects.

Control Wizards Control Wizards help you create **control objects.** Because I don't get into the nitty-gritty details of custom form and report design here, I don't spend much time discussing Control Wizards and control objects—except to explain how you use them to construct **macro buttons** for **forms.**

Converting Access 1.0 Files ⁙ **Database**

Counters A counter is a **field** that Microsoft Access fills for you.
Microsoft Access fills counter fields with sequential numbers. Typically, you use counter fields to assign unique
identification numbers to the **records** in a **table.** In this
case, the counter field is the **primary key** and, most probably, a **common field** if you are joining two tables.

If a counter field is a common field

If you want to use the identification numbers created by a counter
field as the common field between two tables, the identification
number in the other, nonprimary table must have its data type
specified as Long Integer.

Crosstabulation You can crosstabulate data as part of a **query**.
For example, you might run a query that summarizes
product sales by customer in a customer database.

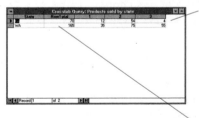

In this crosstabulation,
Access uses rows to
summarize the product
sales by state and
columns to summarize
the sales by product
identification numbers: 1,
2, and 3.

The first column shows
the total products sold in
a state. The row-column
intersections show prod-
uct sales in a state.

A friendly suggestion

Think of a crosstabulation as a query on steroids. It's big. It's powerful. It's not something you want to get into the ring with until you've had a few practice rounds with the simpler select queries in Microsoft Access.

Creating a Crosstab Query

To create a crosstab query, follow these steps:

1 Open the database to which the query should be added.

2 Choose the Query object button.

3 Choose the New command button. Access displays the New Query dialog box.

4 Choose the Query Wizards button. Access displays the Query Wizards dialog box. Make sure the Crosstab Query is selected and click OK.

5 When Access displays the first Crosstab Query Wizard dialog box, indicate whether you want to see tables, queries, or both tables and queries by selecting one of the View option buttons.

6 Select the table or query you'll query by clicking it.

continues

Crosstabulation *(continued)*

7 Choose the Next command button. Microsoft Access displays the second Crosstab Query Wizard dialog box.

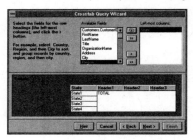

8 Add the field you'll summarize in rows to the crosstabulation summary by selecting it from the list box at the top of the dialog box.

9 Choose Next. Microsoft Access displays the third Crosstab Query Wizard dialog box.

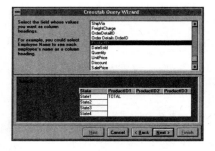

10 Add the fields you'll summarize in columns by selecting them from the list box at the top of the dialog box.

11 Choose Next. Access displays the fourth Crosstab Query Wizard dialog box.

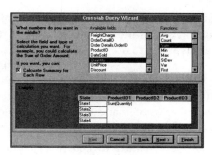

12 Specify what you want to summarize in the crosstabulation by selecting the field you want to summarize and the summary calculation you want to make.

13 Choose Next. Microsoft Access displays the fifth Crosstab Query Wizard dialog box.

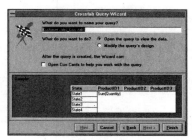

14 Give the crosstab query a name.

15 Choose Finish. Access performs the crosstab query.

Cue Cards Microsoft Access includes a clever, additional type of online assistance, Cue Cards. You can start the Cue Cards feature by choosing the Help Cue Cards command.

.°. Help

Database A database is simply a collection of related information, or data. The real-life database example that books like this always seem to use is a telephone directory. It lists peoples' names, addresses, and telephone numbers; so it's a "names-and-numbers" database. Here's another example: In business, accounting programs create financial databases—lists of financial information such as customer invoices, expenses, and items held as inventory.

In Microsoft Access, the term *database* is defined a bit more precisely. An Access database comprises its database **objects,** or components: **tables, queries, forms, reports, macros,** and **modules.** Access stores the objects that constitute a database in a single **file.**

Creating a New Database File

To create a new database, follow these steps:

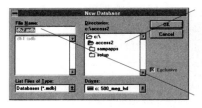

1 Choose the File New Database command.

2 In the Directories list box, specify where the database should be located. (If needed, you can also use the Drives list box.)

3 Enter a filename in the File Name list box.

4 Choose OK.

Opening an Existing Database File

To open a database file that already exists, follow these steps:

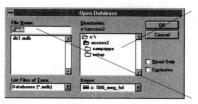

1 Choose the File Open Database command.

2 In the Directories list box, specify where the database is located. (If needed, you can also use the Drives list box.)

3 Enter the filename in the File Name list box.

4 Choose OK.

Using Databases Created with Earlier Versions of Microsoft Access

You'll need to convert databases created with Microsoft Access version 1.0 or 1.1. To do this, first close any open databases and then choose the File Convert Database command. Microsoft Access displays a dialog box you use to identify the to-be-converted database file. You can also rename the database file. (Do this if you don't want the database file conversion to replace the old file with the new file.)

Adding Data to a Database File

Once you've created the database file, you're ready to begin creating tables and filling the tables with data.

⠀RDBMS

Database Window The database window is the window that appears when you open an existing database **file** or create a new database file. It provides **object buttons** that you can click to see the type of database **objects** in your **database.** To see a picture of a database window, turn to pages 4-5.

Datasheet

Microsoft Access uses a datasheet to display **table** records and **query** results on screen. You can enter data directly into a datasheet.

The datasheet's columns show **fields**.

Each datasheet row shows a **record**.

Printing a Datasheet

You can print a datasheet by choosing the File Print command. When Access displays the Print dialog box, use its options to specify how the datasheet should be printed. Or press Enter to accept the default, or suggested, options.

Changing Column Widths

You can change the width of a datasheet's column by dragging the right edge of the column heading. You can also choose the Format Column Width command and enter a column width specification in characters.

Changing the column width automatically

You can tell Access it should adjust a column width to the size of the longest entry by double-clicking on the right edge of the column heading.

Moving Columns

You can move the selected column by dragging it to a new location.

Changing Row Heights

You can change the height of a datasheet's rows by dragging the bottom edge of any row heading. You can also choose the Format Row Height command and enter a row height specification in points. (One point equals 1/72 inch.)

Hiding and Unhiding Columns

You can hide a column so that it doesn't show in a datasheet. To do this, select the column by clicking it, and then choose the Format Hide Columns command.

To unhide columns you've previously hidden, choose the Format Show Columns command. When Access displays the Show Columns dialog box, select columns from the Column list box and then choose Show.

Freezing Columns

You can freeze a column or multiple columns so that they don't scroll off the screen as you scroll right. To do this, select the column by clicking it, and then choose the Format Freeze Columns command.

To unfreeze frozen columns, choose the Format Unfreeze All Columns command.

Data Types Data type refers to the characteristics of the information in a **field**. If the field contains textual information such as someone's first name, it's a text field. Or, stated in a slightly more obtuse manner, the field's data type is text. If a field contains a value that you want (or may want) to use in a calculation, it's a number field. (A field's data type may also limit the type of stuff you can enter.)

Microsoft Access provides you with eight data types, as summarized in the little table that follows:

Data type	What a field of this data type stores
Text	Anything you want as long as the field contains fewer than 255 characters.
Memo	Text—just like the text data type—except that this field holds bigger chunks of text (a maximum of 32,000 characters).
Number	A numeric value that you want (or may want) to use in a calculation. (A number field can't store alphabetic characters. That makes sense, right?)
Currency	A numeric value rounded to two decimal places. (If you're working in the United States, for example, you'll use currency fields to store dollars and cents. If you're working in Great Britain, you'll use currency field fields to store pounds and pence.)
Counter	A numeric value that Access calculates and fills for you by adding one to the previous record's, or table row's, counter. (You use the Counter field when you don't have another numbering scheme or system for uniquely identifying records.)
Date/Time	A calendar and clock value. (Access, you may be in terested to know, automatically validates stuff that you stick into Date/Time fields: Whatever you enter into one of these fields must look like a date or a time.)
Yes/No	A value that can only equal Yes or No. Yes can be indicated as *Yes, True,* or *On.* No can be indicated as *No, False,* or *Off.*
OLE Object	A field that can only hold an OLE object—for example, pictures created by the Paintbrush accessory and sounds created by the Sound Recorder accessory.

⁙ Object Linking and Embedding (OLE); Validation Rules

Why there aren't calculation fields

You don't need fields for storing calculation results. Access will make calculations for you as you need them and then display the results in dynasets produced by queries and on reports and forms.

Default Values When you design and redesign a **table,** you can tell Microsoft Access to suggest a default entry for a **field.** You do this using the Default Value **Field Property**. Here are some examples of default value settings and their effect.

Default value	Microsoft Access suggestion
USA	If the data type is text, Access suggests USA.
1	If the data type is text, Access suggests the character 1. If the data type is number, Access suggests the value 1. If the data type is Yes/No, Access suggests the answer Yes.
0	If the data type is text, Access suggests the character 0. If the data type is number, Access suggests the value 0. If the data type is Yes/No, Access suggests the answer No.
=Date()	If the data type is Date/Time, Access suggests the current system date.
=Time()	If the data type is Date/Time, Access suggests the current system time.
=Now()	If the data type is Date/Time, Access suggests the current system date and time.

Expressions; Functions

Deleting Files ❖ **Erasing Databases**

Documents In Windows-based applications, a document is what gets displayed in the **document window** that an **application** displays. In the case of a word processor, this name works pretty nicely. The report, letter, or memo that a word processor displays in a document window inside its application is, well, basically a document. Right?

Unfortunately, the "document" label doesn't work as well when it's used to name the windows and window contents that Microsoft Access displays. What Access displays in the windows inside its application window are **views** of the database **objects.** Nevertheless, Access still labels these objects and object views as documents. For example, when you choose the File Print command, Access tells you (via the status bar) that it prints the document.

Document Window A document window is the window in which an **application** such as Access displays the **views** of its database **objects.**

Dynaset Dynaset is a shorthand expression for "dynamic subset." When you query a **table** or a **query,** what gets displayed in the **datasheet window** is a dynamic subset, or a dynaset. (We'll use the term now since we both understand it, OK?)

What makes a dynaset "dynamic" is this: If you make a change to the information displayed in the datasheet window (because of the query), Access updates the tables that provided the raw information.

E

Embedding and Linking Objects

Microsoft Access lets you store more than numbers and chunks of text in **tables.** It also lets you store OLE (**Object Linking and Embedding**) objects. (This is confusing, but just for the record, these OLE objects are different from the **objects** that constitute a database.)

Embedding and Linking Existing Objects

To create an object from an existing file, follow these steps:

1 Place the insertion point in the **field** into which the object should be inserted. (Note that the field's **data type** must be "OLE Object.")

2 Choose the Edit Insert Object command.

3 Choose the Create from File button.

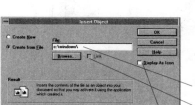

4 Describe the object file location.

5 Identify the object file.

6 Mark the Link check box if Windows should update the object for subsequent file changes.

7 Mark the Display As Icon check box if Access should display an icon to represent the embedded object rather than a picture.

8 Choose OK.

continues

Embedding and Linking Objects *(continued)*

Embedding New Objects

To create an object from scratch, follow these steps:

1 Place the insertion point in the field into which the object should be inserted. (Sorry to be obsessive, but note again that the field's data type must be "OLE Object.")

2 Choose the Edit Insert Object command.

3 Select the Create New option.

4 Select the Windows-based application that creates the object.

5 Mark the Display As Icon check box to see the embedded object as an icon rather than as a picture.

6 Choose OK. Access starts the selected application, allowing you to create the object.

7 When you're done, exit the application.

Entering Text and Numbers

To enter text or numbers into a form's text box or a datasheet's cell, select the box or cell by clicking or by pressing the Tab key. Then use the keyboard to type the characters. You can enter special **ANSI characters** too, as long as you know the ANSI character code.

In Access, you edit and erase text and numbers the same way you do in other Windows-based applications. Note, though, that you may be limited as to what you can enter into a text box or cell by the field's **data type.**

Equi-Join

When Microsoft Access joins **tables** in a multiple-table **query,** it runs something called an equi-join. Basically, what this means is that you won't see query results unless Access can successfully join records in all the tables. For example, if you're joining customer table **records** and customer order table records, Access won't show customer order records for customers that don't exist in the customer table. Usually, this is what you want. You should know, however, that you can also run something called an **outer-join**.

❖ **Self-Join**

Erasing Databases

Erasing Databases **Databases** get stored as files on disk. To erase them in the Windows operating environment, you use the File Manager application.

 Program Manager > Main > File Manager

Erasing Files with File Manager

To erase a file once you've started File Manager, follow these steps:

1 Select the directory or the subdirectory that contains the file or files you want to erase.

2 Select the file or files you want to erase.

3 Choose the File Delete command.

4 When File Manager asks, confirm that you do want to delete the file.

What's in a database file?

A database file contains all the objects that make up the database. It doesn't contain tables that are only attached, however.

 Object

Exiting Microsoft Access

Exiting Microsoft Access To exit from Access (and just about any other Windows-based application), you can choose the File Exit command. Or you can close the **application window**—for example, by double-clicking on its Control-menu box. Access will ask if you want to save **objects** that have unsaved changes. Note that Access automatically saves changes to table **records** and new records.

Closing Database Objects; Saving Databases and Objects

Exiting Windows

Exiting Windows To exit from Microsoft Windows, choose Program Manager's File Exit Windows command or close the Program Manager window. When you exit from Windows, Windows closes any Windows-based applications that are running.

Exiting Microsoft Access

Exporting Data You can export data from Microsoft Access and use it in a spreadsheet such as Microsoft Excel or in a word processor such as Microsoft Word. You can do this in a variety of ways, but here's the easiest and most expeditious:

1 Prepare a **report** that shows the data you want to export in the way you want it exported. Or open the **table** with the data you want to export.

2 Choose the File Output To command. Access displays the first Output To dialog box.

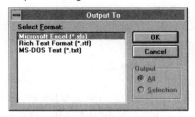

3 Select an output format that can be imported by the **application** you'll later use to work with the data. (Use Rich Text Format for exporting to a word processor like Microsoft Word.)

4 Choose OK. Access displays the second Output To dialog box.

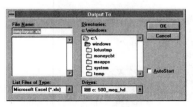

5 Enter a filename for the new exported file.

6 Use the Directories and Drives list boxes to specify where the file should be located.

7 Choose OK.

Exporting Data *(continued)*

Outputting to Microsoft Excel or to Microsoft Word

You can use the Output to Excel and Output to Word tools, which appear on the toolbar when a report is displayed, to export reports to Microsoft Excel and Microsoft Word.

Expressions An expression is simply a formula. You can use expressions to return **default values** for input fields in **datasheets** and **forms.** You can use expressions for **calculated fields** in **queries.** You can use expressions to validate field entries. And you can even use expressions in **Access Basic** modules.

⁂ **Modules; Validation Rules**

Field   The columns in a **table** are called fields. Each field stores the same type of information. For example, you might have a street address column in a customer names and addresses table; so street address is a field. Note, though, that each customer would almost certainly have a unique street address. Mr. Holmes may live at 22B Baker Street, for example, while Professor Moriarty lives at 40 Kensington.

A curious but very powerful feature of Access is that it doesn't limit you to storing only text and numbers in fields. You can also store OLE objects. This means you can put a picture in a **database,** for example. And it means you can put another application's **document** in a database.

⁂ **Object Linking and Embedding (OLE); Objects**

Field Names   You name **fields** when you create a **table.** You can use as many as 64 characters for a field name—including all letters and numbers and most special characters. (You can't use periods, exclamation points, or brackets.) You can use blank spaces if you want, but you can't start a field name with a blank space.

Naming fields

Although you can use spaces in field names, it's better if you don't. Field names without spaces are usually easier to use in expressions and are easier to export.

⁂ **Expressions**

Field Property When you define a table column, or **field,** you name it and assign a **data type** to it. If you're the diligent sort, you may want to add a description that shows on the status bar whenever the field is selected. (This last step really is a good idea.) You can describe a field in more detail than this, however, by using the field property boxes at the bottom of the Table window when it shows the Design view of a table.

Changing Field Properties

To change a field property, first select the field. Typically, Access adds an arrow button just to the right of the property box. You can click this arrow to activate a drop-down list box of the property settings available for the selected field.

Changing the Field Size Property for a Text Field

The Text and Memo Field Size property tells Access how many characters can go into a field. You simply click the Field Size box and enter a number. A text field needs to be long enough to hold the full range of possible entries (or reasonable abbreviations). But don't make a text field longer than is necessary. Doing so makes it possible for someone to enter an incorrectly long entry.

Field size and disk space

You don't use up extra space by setting the field size to a big number. For example, if you set a field used for storing 2-character state abbreviations to 50 characters in length but only enter 2-character state abbreviations into the field, Access stores the field contents on disk in 2-character chunks, not 50-character chunks. Access can do this because it uses something called the Indexed Sequential Access Method for storing data.

Changing the Field Size Property for Number and Counter Fields

The Field Size property tells Access how large a value can go in the field. Here are your choices:

Field Size	Range of values field can hold
Byte	Integers from 0 to 255
Integer	Integers from -32768 to 32767
Long integer	Integers from -2,147,483,648 to 2,147,483,647. (Yikes.)
Single	Values with 7 decimal places from -3.4×10^{38} to 3.4×10^{38}
Double	Values with 15 decimal places from -1.797×10^{308} to 1.797×10^{308}. (Double Yikes.)

Choose the smallest size that works

The bigger the numbers that fit in a field, the more room the field takes. The Byte field size, for example, takes only a single byte. (I wonder if that isn't where it got its name, eh?) The Integer size takes 2 bytes, the Long Integer and Single sizes take 4 bytes, and the Double size takes 8 bytes.

Changing the Format of Number, Counter, and Currency Fields

If the selected field is a number, a counter, or a currency field, you can select the Format box and choose an entry from the Format drop-down list box. The number formats are all pretty self-explanatory, but if you have a question, just experiment a bit.

Changing the Format of a Date/Time Field

Access lets you display dates in a variety of formats too. Long dates, short dates, fat dates, skinny dates—wait a minute. Forget those last two. Wrong book. But you get the idea, right?

continues

Field Property *(continued)*

Changing the Format of a Yes/No Field

Yes/No fields can hold any of the following three sets of answers: Yes or No, True or False, or On or Off. You choose which set of answers are valid for the field by selecting the Yes/No field and then using the Format drop-down list box.

Creating an Input Mask

You can create an input mask for a field. An input mask helps you enter information into a field in a predefined format. For example, if you want to store the telephone number *2065551234* as *(206) 555-1234,* you can create an input mask that adds the parentheses, space, and hyphen. To create an input mask for the selected field, click the Input Mask property text box and then click the button that appears just right of the property text box. Doing so starts the Input Mask Wizard, which steps you through the process of creating an input mask.

Specifying Decimal Places for Number and Currency Fields

You can specify how many decimal places Access should use to display a field's value using the Decimal Places property. To use the same number of decimal places as the format, select the Auto entry from the Decimal Places drop-down list box. When the format you've selected for a field is general, the Decimal Places property has no effect.

Adding a Caption

A caption is what Access uses to label input blanks—text boxes, really—on the **forms** you use to collect field data and on **reports** that summarize the data. To add a caption, fill in the Caption property box. The Caption field, as you might guess, works the same for all data types.

Suggesting Default Text or Value Entries for Fields

You can suggest an entry for a field by filling in the Default Value property box. You can enter a chunk of text, a number, or an **expression** that returns a value.

If you were building a names and addresses table and figured that most of the addresses would use US as the country, you might use the text "US" as the default value for the country field.

You can also specify a default value for a number field.

You can also enter a formula, or expression, that returns a value. For example, the expression =DATE() plugs the current system date into a field as the default entry. Date(), by the way, is only one of the functions you can use in Access.

Validating Field Entries

You can tell Access it should validate field entries too. To do this, you enter **validation rules**.

Validation Error Messages

If you specify a validation rule for a field, you can use the Validation message box to input the message that a user sees in a message box if a field entry doesn't pass the validation test.

Why You Should be Careful When Setting Field Properties

Forms and reports that you create for viewing or changing data from the table inherit many of the properties. For example, if you specify a validation rule for a field, Access uses the rule to check the data you enter into a form.

File

Applications such as the Windows File Manager and Access get stored on your disk as files. The **databases** you create in Access—including all the **objects** that constitute the database—also get stored on disk as files. In general, you manipulate files—even database files—with File Manager, and you manipulate the contents of the database files—table records, for example—with Access.

Filenames
You give a **database** its filename when you choose the File New Database command.

File-Naming Rules
MS-DOS file-naming rules apply to Microsoft Access database files. A filename can't have more than eight characters. All numbers and letters that appear on your keyboard are OK. And so are many other characters. You can't, however, use characters that MS-DOS expects to be used in special ways on its command line, such as spaces, asterisks, and question marks. If you need more information, refer to the MS-DOS user documentation that almost surely came with your computer.

When MS-DOS File-Naming Rules Don't Apply
The MS-DOS file-naming rules apply only to the database file. They don't apply to the **objects** that make up a database. You aren't limited to eight characters, for example, in naming **tables, queries,** and **reports** because these are database objects.

Specifying File Extensions
The file extension, by the way, isn't something you need to worry about. Microsoft Access adds the file extension MDB to identify file type as a Microsoft Access database file.

Object

Filter

A filter is a set of selection criteria, or sorting specifications, that you use to limit and to organize the records displayed in a form or a datasheet. If you're in the process of designing a query, you don't need to create a filter. You can enter the selection criteria as part of designing the query.

 Creating a Filter

To create a filter, first display the form or the datasheet that contains the records you want to filter. Then choose the Records Edit Filter/Sort command or select the Edit Filter/Sort tool. When Access displays the Filter design view window, indicate the field you'll use to sort, the sort order, and any selection criteria.

Specifying fields, sort orders, and selection criteria for a filter works in the same manner as specifying fields, sort orders, and selection criteria for a query.

 Using a Filter

To use a filter you've just created, choose the Records Apply Filter/ Sort command or select the Apply Filter/Sort tool.

 Unfiltering Records

To unfilter the records, choose the Records Show All Records command or select the Show All Records tool.

Finding Records To find a specific record, display a form or
display the datasheet for the table that stores the record.
Then choose the Edit Find command or select the
Find tool.

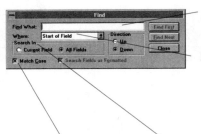

1 In the Find What text
box, specify what
you're looking for.

2 Use the Where drop-
down list box to tell
Access whether what
you're looking for
starts the field, is
somewhere within the
field, or makes up the
entire field.

3 Use the Search In buttons to indicate
whether Access
should search only the
current field or all the
fields. (Searching only
the current field is
faster, but you need to
make sure the insertion
point is in the field
that contains the data.)

4 Use the Direction buttons to specify which
direction Access
should search, or look.

5 Use the Match Case
check box to indicate
whether Access
should consider case
(lower vs. upper) in its
search. (Normally, Ac-
cess ignores case.)

6 Choose Find Next to
start and restart the
search.

Searching for Formatting

Use the Search Fields as Formatted check box to indicate whether
Access should consider the field's formatting in its search. (Normally,
Access ignores formatting.)

Wildcards

You can use wildcard characters in your Find What entry.
The ? character can be used to represent any single character. The * character can be used to represent any single
character or combination of characters. The # character can
be used to represent any combination of digits.

⁂ Wildcard Characters

Foreign Key
A foreign key is the **common field** in a related
table. A primary key, in comparison, is the common field
in the **primary table.**

Forms
A form lets you enter, edit, and view table and query data.

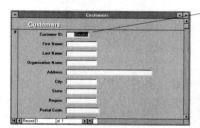

On a form, each field
gets its own text box.
You can design forms
that use other elements
of the Windows
interface: check boxes,
radio buttons, list boxes,
and so on. To use these
other elements, however,
you'll need to design a
form from scratch.

continues

Forms *(continued)*

Creating a Form with the Form Wizards

To create a form using the Form Wizards, follow these steps:

1 Open the database to which the form should be added. Access displays the Database window.

2 Choose the Form object button.

3 Choose the New command button. Access displays the New Form dialog box.

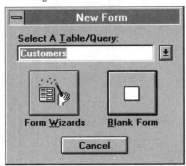

4 Activate the Select A Table/Query drop-down list box and select the object upon which the form should be based.

5 Choose the Form Wizards command button. This tells Access that you want it to do most of the work of setting up the form. Access displays the Form Wizards dialog box, which asks which Wizard you want to use.

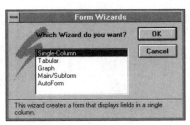

6 Select the Single-Column entry to create a form that displays one record at a time with the record's fields arranged in a single column. (You can also select the Tabular Wizard entry to create a form that displays several records in a form that resembles a datasheet.) Click OK. Access displays the Single-Column Form Wizard dialog box.

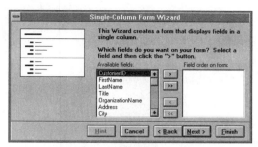

7 Select the fields you want in the order they should appear on the form. You can select individual table fields by clicking the field in the Available fields list box and then choosing the > button. You can select all the table's fields by choosing the >> button. You can remove a field from the Field order on form list box by clicking it and choosing <. You can remove all the fields from the Field order on form list box by choosing the << button.

8 Choose Next. Access displays another Single-Column Form Wizard dialog box. This one asks how you want your form to look.

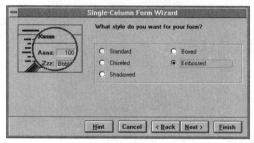

9 Choose the option button that corresponds to the "look" you want. Of course, if this is the first time you've done this, you won't know which looks are which, so take a gander at the magnifying glass. It'll show how the various "looks" look.

10 Choose Next. Access displays yet another Single-Column Form Wizard dialog box. This one asks what name Access should use for the form and whether you want to start using the form or want to instead redesign some of the form by fiddling with its **control objects.** You can replace the suggested name if you want. But you probably needn't worry about redesigning the form—especially if you're in a hurry.

continues

Forms *(continued)*

11 When you're done, choose the Finish command button. Access displays your new form.

Editing Data with a Form

Initially, Access shows the first table record in the form. (If there aren't any records in the table or query, the form's boxes are blank.) To edit a record, first display it. You can move back and forth through the table's records by using the PageUp and PageDown keys. You can move back and forth through the form's fields with the Tab and Shift-Tab keys.

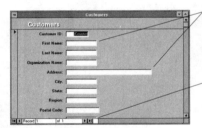

Once you've displayed the record you want to change, make your changes by replacing or editing text boxes.

You can also use these buttons to move back and forth through a table's records. The < and > buttons move to the previous or next record. The |< and >| buttons move to the first or last record.

Entering Data into a Form

To enter a new record into a table using a form, choose the >l button to display the last record in the table and then choose the > button to display a new, empty record. Alternatively, choose the Record Go To New command. Either way, Access displays a blank form. All you do is fill in the blanks.

Making Simple Form Design Changes

You can do a lot of very tricky, rather clever things with your form design. Here, however, I'm only going to describe one change: rearranging the text boxes on the form. To do this, display the form (if it isn't already displayed) and then select the Design View tool.

When Access displays the design view of the form, drag the boxes around the screen using the mouse.

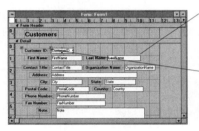

To move both the box and its description together, select either object and then drag.

To move the box or the description independently, select either object and then drag the large selection handle in the top left corner of the description or the box.

Printing Forms

To print forms for all the records in a table or a query or to print only the record currently displayed in the form, follow these steps:

1 Display the form.

2 Choose the File Print command. Access displays the Print dialog box.

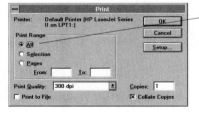

3 Select the All option if you want to print all the records, or select the Selection option if you want to print only the displayed record.

4 Choose OK.

continues

Forms *(continued)*

Closing a Form

When you finish entering or editing information in a form, close the form by double-clicking its Control-menu box. Or choose the File Close command.

If you haven't closed the form before, Access asks if you want to save it. You probably do, right? So choose Yes. Access next presents a dialog box you can use to give the form a more useful name than Form1. You can (and should) do this.

Using an Existing Form

To use a form you've already created, open the database, choose the Form object button, and then double-click the form. Access then displays the Form.

 Autoform; Graphs; Object Names; Primary Key; Printing

Functions

Functions are prefabricated formulas that you use in **expressions** and in **Access Basic** modules. Microsoft Access provides functions that perform financial, mathematical, and statistical calculations.

Functions in Microsoft Access closely resemble functions in Microsoft Excel

Many functions in Microsoft Access work like those in a spreadsheet. If you've used functions in Microsoft Excel or in Lotus 1-2-3, you'll find using functions in Microsoft Access easy and straightforward.

Modules

Graphs Microsoft Access comes with the Microsoft Graph application. Graph, as it's called by those who know it well, lets
you easily create charts based on information shown in a
table or a **query.** You can add graphs to **reports** and
forms, but if you just want a quick-and-dirty chart, the
easiest way to do this is to create a form using the Graph
Wizard. Basically, to do this, you simply tell Microsoft
Access which table or query holds the data you want to
plot and how you want the data charted.

For Microsoft Excel users

In Access, the Graph Wizard—which is the wizard that creates a
graph—is almost identical to the Chart Wizard in Microsoft Excel.
If you've created a chart in Microsoft Excel you'll find creating a
graph in Access as easy as shooting fish in a barrel.

Help   Windows itself and almost all Windows-based applications (which is what Microsoft Access is) include an
online help feature, which means means information is
almost always just a click or a keystroke away. You access
this help by using one of the Help menu commands.

I'm not going to get into the intricacies of Windows Help
here. But if you're not familiar with how Help works, take
the time to get to know this handy tool. You'll be glad you
did.

Getting Help in Microsoft Access

Need help, say, with some Microsoft Access task? No problem. Select
the Help toolbar button. The **application** adds a question mark to the
mouse pointer arrow.

To indicate what you want help with, click the item. After you select
the item, the application starts Help. It displays any specific
information about what you selected.

Importing Data You can import data stored in a table file that
is external to Microsoft Access either by attaching the
table with the data to an existing **database** or by actually
importing the file into Access. (When you attach a table,
the data stays in the other, external file. When you import
the file, it becomes a table **object** in an Access database file.)

Attaching an External Table

To attach an external table to the open Access database, follow these steps:

1 Choose the File Attach Table command.

2 Identify the data source type and choose OK.

3 When Access displays the Select File dialog box, identify the file by giving its disk and directory location and its name. (This dialog box works like the one you use to open a database file.)

4 When Access displays the Attach Table dialog box, identify the table and select Attach.

Importing a Table

To import a table into Microsoft Access, follow these steps:

1 Choose the File Import command.

2 Identify the data source type and choose OK.

3 When Access displays the Select File dialog box, identify the file by giving its disk and directory location and its name. (This dialog box works like the one you use to open a database file.)

4 When Access displays the Attach Table dialog box, identify the table and select Import.

Which database files you can import

Which database files you can import depends on which database drivers you installed as part and parcel of setting up Microsoft Access.

Index   A database index works in a manner similar to a library's
card catalog. A library's card catalog (whether it's still on
those little paper cards we all know and love or whether
it's on a computer) provides a list of the books in the library and their locations. By looking through the card
catalog, you save yourself the trouble (and the time) of
having to search every shelf in every bookcase on every
floor of the library.

In the same manner, a database index provides a list of
the **records** in a **table** and their disk location. An index
makes querying a database much faster because Access
has to search only the index (which resides or mostly resides in memory) rather than each of the individual
records (which reside on your disk).

If you've created a **primary key** for a table, it becomes the
index. If you haven't created a primary key, Access asks if
it can add an index when you save the table. If you answer, "Yeah, man," it does, calling the index something
clever and descriptive (usually, "counter"). If you answer
"No way, man," your table doesn't have an index. And if
the table gets big, you'll have a heck of a time searching it.

Adding a Single-Field Index

You can add a single-field index to a table by following these steps:

1 Open the database if it isn't already open.

2 Choose the Table object button.

3 Select the table and then choose the Design button. Access
displays the Design View window for the table object.

4 Select the field you want to use for the index.

5 Select the Indexed field property.

6 Activate the Index drop-down list box and select either the Yes
(No Duplicates) or Yes (Duplicates OK) entry.

Removing an Index

If you make a mistake in assigning an index, you can remove it. Here's how:

1 Open the database if it isn't already open.

2 Choose the Table object button.

3 Select the table and then choose the Design button. Access displays the Design View window for the table object.

4 Select the field.

5 Select the Indexed field property.

6 Activate the Index drop-down list box and choose No.

Adding a Multiple-Field Index

You can add a multiple-field index to a table too. You might do this if you find yourself frequently sorting based on several fields. By creating a multiple-field key, you increase the speed of the sort operation.

1 Open the database if it isn't already open.

2 Choose the Table object button.

3 Select the table and then choose the Design button. Access displays the Design View window for the table object.

4 Choose the View Indexes command.

5 Select the first open row in the Indexes grid.

6 Use the Index Name column to label the index.

7 Use the Field Name column to enter the field names that should constitute the index in the order in which they should be used to sort: primary key, secondary key, tertiary key, and so on. Separate the field names by entering them onto different rows.

8 Close the Indexes dialog box when you finish.

9 Close the Design View window for the table object. When Access asks if you want to save your changes, choose Yes.

Joining Tables
When you want to combine two or more **tables** in a single **query,** Microsoft Access "joins" them. Join is really a database buzzword, so you can think about joins as combinations.

If you've defined a **relationship** between the two tables, Access already knows how to join, or combine, them. When you add both tables to the query, Access draws a join line between the table's **common fields**. (This is really the best way to proceed, so let me respectfully suggest you flip to the **Relationships** entry to see how this relationship-building business works.)

If you haven't defined a relationship, you can tell Access how it should join the tables as part of setting up the query. To do this, select the common field in the **primary table**—for example, by clicking it—and then drag it to the common field in the related table. (To delete a join, select the join line that Access adds and then press the Del key.)

Joining tables that don't share a common field
You can join tables that don't share a common field by including a third table that has common fields for the other two tables. In this case, you might be able to connect table 1 to table 2 with one common field and then connect table 2 to table 3 with another common field. Once this is done, you can combine, or join, table 1 and table 3 in a query.

Equi-Join; Outer-Join; Self-Join

Keyboard Navigation
You can use the keyboard to move through the **records** in a **table**, through the **fields** in a record, and through the characters in a field text box. How you can navigate with the keyboard is good stuff to know; so here's a list of the most useful techniques.

Key	What it does
Up	Moves selection cursor to previous record in a datasheet or to the previous field in a form
Down	Moves selection cursor to the next record in a datasheet or the next field in a form
Left	Moves insertion point one character left
Right	Moves insertion point one character right. A big surprise to you, no doubt.
Ctrl+Up	Moves selection cursor to top of column, or to the same field in the first record shown in a datasheet
Ctrl+Down	Moves selection cursor to bottom of column, or to the same field in the last record shown in a datasheet
Ctrl+Left	Moves insertion point one word left
Ctrl+Right	Moves insertion point one word right. Another big surprise to you, no doubt.
Tab	Moves selection to cursor to next field
Shift+Tab	Moves selection cursor to the previous field
Enter	Moves selection cursor to the next field
Ctrl+Enter	Hey. This is rather handy. It ends a line of text in a Memo field.
PgUp	Scrolls up what's shown in the window
PgDn	Scrolls down what's shown in the window
Ctrl+PgUp	Scrolls left what's shown in the window
Ctrl+PgDn	Scrolls right what's shown in the window
Home	Moves selection cursor to the first field in a record
End	Moves selection cursor to the last field in a record
Ctrl+Home	Moves selection cursor to first field in a table
Ctrl+End	Moves selection cursor to last field in a table

continues

Keyboard Navigation *(continued)*

Differentiating the Insertion Point and the Selection Cursor

The insertion point is the vertical bar that shows where what you type gets placed. If you can't figure this out, start a Windows-based **application** such as Write, begin typing, and look at the bar that moves ahead of the text you type. See it? That's the insertion point.

The selection cursor is the thing that marks the selected option on a dialog box or the selected text in a box or the selected row in a datasheet. How Microsoft Windows marks objects with the selection cursor depends on the object being marked.

Navigating with the mouse

You can move around a table, a form, or a text box by clicking what you want to select. That's right. Just click it.

Logical Operators

You can use logical operators to construct logical **expressions** for **validation rules** and to construct selection criteria for **queries.** Here's a table that describes and illustrates these powerful tools.

Operator	Description and example
=	This is the equals operator. If you enter the logical expression *=100* as a validation rule for the Deposit field, you've said that a deposit must equal 100.
>	This is the greater than operator. If you enter the logical expression *>100* as a validation rule for the Deposit field, you've said that a deposit must be greater than 100.
<	This is the less than operator. If you enter the logical expression *<100* as a validation rule for the Deposit field, you've said that a deposit must be less than 100.
>=	This is the greater than or equal to operator. If you enter the logical expression *>=100* as validation rule for the Deposit field, you've said that a deposit must be greater than or equal to 100.
<=	This is the less than or equal to operator. If you enter the logical expression *<=100* as a validation rule for the Deposit field, you've said that a deposit must be less than or equal to 100.

Operator   Description and example

Operator	Description and example
<>	This is the not equal to operator. If you enter the logical expression <>*100* as a validation rule for the Deposit field, you've said that a deposit must not equal 100.
And	This operator combines expressions. For the combined expression to be true, each of the component expressions must be true. If you enter the logical expression *>100 And < 500* as a validation rule for the Deposit field, you've said that a deposit must be greater than 100 and less than 500. (In other words, the deposit must fall within the range of 100 to 500.)
Or	This operator combines expressions. For the combined expression to be true, any one of the component expressions must be true. If you enter the logical expression *<100 Or > 500* as a validation rule for the Deposit field, you've said that a deposit must be either less than 100 or greater than 500.
Not	This operator negates an expression. If you enter the logical expression *Not <100* as a validation rule for the Deposit field, you've said that a deposit must not be less than 100. For the record, mathematicians and programmers used "Not!" long before Wayne and Garth.
Between	This operator tests whether a value falls within a range. If you enter the logical expression *Between 100 And 500* as a validation rule for the Deposit field, you've said that a deposit must equal or exceed 100 but can't exceed 500.
In	This operator tests whether an entry is an item in a set. If you enter the logical expression *In (50 100 200)* as a validation rule for the Deposit field, you've said that a deposit must equal 50 or 100 or 200.
Is Null	This expression tests whether a field is empty. You wouldn't use this operator as a validation rule. You might use it as a selection criterion to find records with an empty Deposit field.
Is Not Null	This expression tests whether a field isn't empty. You might use it to find records with something entered in the Deposit field.
Like	This expression tests whether the entry in a text field matches a pattern. If you enter the logical expression *Like ??* as a validation rule for a State field, you've said that the State must equal two characters. If you know the State field entry should start with the letter C, you would enter the expression as *Like C?*.

Macro Buttons A macro button is a **control object** that you can add to a **form.** As cool as control objects are, they're often too involved for the lightning quick solutions this little book is supposed to provide. But there is an exception: macro button control objects. You can add a macro button to a form to automate some repetitive task related to using the form.

Creating a Macro Button

To create a macro button, follow these steps:

1 Display the form to which the macro button should be added.

 2 Select the Design View tool so that Access displays the Design View window for the form object. Access displays the design view of the **object** and the **Toolbox.** (If Access doesn't display the toolbox, choose the View Toolbox command.)

 3 Select the Control Wizards tool in the Toolbox, if it isn't already depressed.

 4 Select the Command Button tool.

5 Place and size the command button on the form by clicking the top left corner and then dragging the mouse to the bottom right corner where you want the command button. When you release the mouse button, Access displays the first Command Button Wizard dialog box.

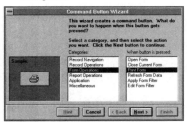

6 Use the Categories and When button is pressed list boxes to indicate what you want Access to do when you click the command button. As you select different categories, of course, Access changes the actions listed in the When button is pressed list box.

7 Choose Next. Access displays the second Command Button Wizard dialog box.

8 Provide Access with the additional information it needs to complete the action you identified in step 6. For example, if you said you wanted Access to print a form when you click the command button, Access asks, "Which form would you like this button to print?"

9 Choose Next. Access displays the third Command Button Wizard dialog box.

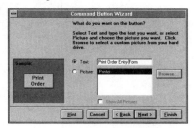

10 Describe how the button should look. You can provide a textual label for the command button or specify that a picture (such as of a printer) should be used.

continues

Macro Buttons *(continued)*

11 Choose Next. Access displays the fourth and final Command Button Wizard dialog box.

12 Name the command button control object. Marge. Al. Desmond. Or perhaps something more clever. By the way, if you wanted to write **Access Basic** modules that act on control objects, you would use the name you assign in this step.

13 Choose Finish. Access adds the command button to the form.

14 Choose the File Save command to save the form design changes. Then choose the File Close command to close the form design view window.

⁞⁝ **Modules**

Macros A macro is simply a list of commands. Microsoft Access lets you store these lists and repeat, or play back, the stored commands. With this play-back ability, you can automate operations that work the same way every time they are performed.

⁞⁝ **Macro Buttons**

Mailing Labels If you've stored names and addresses in a **table** or created a **query** that produces a names and addresses **dynaset**, you can easily create mailing labels. (Mailing labels, just for the record, are a type of **report**.)

Creating a Mailing Labels Report

To do so, follow these steps:

1 Open the **database** to which the report should be added. Access displays the Database window.

2 Choose the Report object button.

3 Choose the New command button. Access displays the New Report dialog box.

4 Activate the drop-down list box and select the table or query that holds the mailing list information—names, street addresses, and so on.

5 Choose the Report Wizards command button. This tells Access that you want it to do most of the work of setting up the mailing list report. Access displays the Report Wizards dialog box, which asks which Microsoft Access Wizard you want to use.

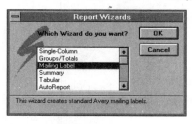

6 Select Mailing Label.

continues

Mailing Labels *(continued)*

7 Choose OK. Access displays the first Mailing Label Wizard dialog box.

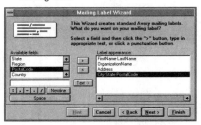

8 Select the **field** you want to appear on the first line of the mailing label and then choose the > button. (To remove a field, choose the < button.)

9 If you want a space or some punctuation to follow the field you just added, choose one of the punctuation buttons. (To remove punctuation, choose the < button.)

10 If you want the next field to appear on the next line, choose the New Line button.

11 Repeat steps 8, 9, and 10 to add additional fields, punctuation, and spacing to the mailing label. The Label appearance box shows, approximately, how your label will look.

12 Choose Next. Access displays another Mailing Label Wizard dialog box. This one asks how you want your mailing labels sorted.

13 Select the first field that you want Access to use for alphabetizing or arranging fields by clicking it and then choosing the > button. If needed, select another field to alphabetize or arrange table records with the same first field in the same manner. You can remove a field from the Sort order list box by clicking it and choosing <. If you want to start over, remove all the fields from the Sort order list box by choosing the << button.

14 Choose Next. Access displays the third Mailing Label Wizard dialog box. This one asks what size mailing label you're using.

15 Select the size you're using.

16 Choose Next. Access displays a dialog box that asks for your font and color choices.

17 Choose the font and color you want for the labels using the boxes and buttons provided.

18 Choose Next. Access displays a dialog box that tells you you're done and asks if you want to see how your mailing labels look or if you want to open the report design view. Make your choice and then choose the Finish command button.

continues

Mailing Labels *(continued)*

Printing Mailing Labels

To print mailing labels, follow these steps:

1 Preview the mailing labels report in the Print Preview window.

2 Choose the File Print command or select the Print tool. Access displays the Print dialog box.

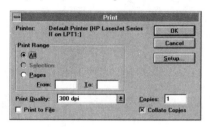

3 Complete the Print dialog box as needed.

Closing a Mailing Labels Report

When you finish reviewing the information in a mailing labels list, or report, close the report by double-clicking its Control-menu box. Or choose the File Close command.

If you haven't closed the mailing labels list before, Access asks if you want to save it. If you indicate you do, Access presents a dialog box you can use to give the mailing labels list a descriptive name. I don't know. How about "mailing labels"?

Using an Existing Mailing Labels List

To use a mailing labels list you've already created, open the database, choose the Reports object button, and then double-click the mailing labels list or choose the Preview command button. Access displays the mailing labels list in a Print Preview window.

Main Form ⁚⁚ Subform

Mathematical Operators

You can use eight mathematical operators to build calculated field formulas in Access. Here's a table that describes and illustrates these operators:

Operator	What it does
+	Adds values. For example, the expression 2+2 returns the not-surprising result of 4.
-	Subtracts one value from another. For example, the expression 10-2 subtracts 2 from 10, returning 8.
*	Multiplies values. The expression 2*3 returns 6, for example.
/	Divides values. The expression 10/3, for example, returns the 3.333. (How many decimal places those 3s extend will depend on the Number field's format, which determines its decimal precision.)
\	Divides values and returns the integer portion of the dividend. The expression 10\3, for example, returns 3.
Mod	Divides values and returns the remainder. The expression Mod (10,3) returns 1.
^	Raises a value to a specified power. The expression 10^3 raises 10 to the third power, returning 1000.
&	Concatenates strings of text. For example, the expression Walla&Walla returns WallaWalla. I guess, to be darn technical about it, the & operator doesn't do anything mathematical. Access, though, calls it a mathematical operator. So I will too. I don't want to rock the boat.

Operator precedence

Access applies the standard rules of operator precedence in a formula that uses more than one operator: Exponential operations are performed first, then division and multiplication, and then addition and subtraction. You can override these standard rules by using parentheses; Microsoft Access will first perform operations inside parentheses.

∴ Expressions; Query; Validation Rules

Modules A module, another type of database object, is an **Access Basic** program. This book is too tiny to cover Access Basic programs. Sorry.

Normalization Normalization is something that a database designer—this could be you, by the way—does when organizing **fields** into **tables**. Normalizing a database means eliminating repetitive fields within a table and minimizing data redundancy across the tables in the **database.**

For example, let's say you build a database of students and their test scores. Rather than have one table with a bunch of test score fields in it—this is repetition—you would create a test scores table in which each test and test score goes into its own record, or row. And rather than have, for example, the student's full name and address stored in a bunch of different tables—this is data redundancy—you would store the student's name and address in only one place. (You would probably store student names and addresses in a names and addresses table.)

Go ahead and use the word *normalization* as you talk database shop with your friends. It's a good word. And it's a word that makes it sound like you know a lot about database design.

Object The word *object* is an imprecise and extremely confusing term when you're talking about Access. (Well, at least it's extremely confusing to me.) The problem is that the word *object* refers to three, completely different things.

Database Objects

The **tables, queries, forms, reports, macros,** and **modules** that make up a database, for example, are all objects. In other words, the major building blocks of an Access database are called objects. (I'll always call these objects "database objects.")

Control Objects

The things Access places on a form or a report—chunks of text, numbers, calculated amounts, and so on—are called objects too. I don't talk about control objects, except for macro buttons, all that much in this book because you can use the Control Wizard to place and position control objects on a form or a report. (I'll always call these objects "control objects.")

OLE Objects

A third type of object in Access is an embedded or linked object. OLE objects can be stored in fields.

∴ **Object Linking and Embedding**

Object Buttons

Object buttons are those command-button-like things that run along the edge of the database window. You click an object button to display a list of the database objects in that category.

Click the Table object button, for example, to display a list of the table objects in the database.

Object Linking and Embedding (OLE) Object linking and embedding, or OLE, is a Microsoft Windows feature.

What OLE Does

You use it to create what's called a compound document. In the case of Access, a compound document is a database file that uses another application's file or parts of another application's file. A good example of how this works is in the sample Northwinds database that comes with Access. The employees table includes an OLE object field. This field is used to store pictures of employees—such as might be created by the Windows Paintbrush application. (Note that Access doesn't let you create picture fields.) In a nutshell, then, a compound document really consists of stuff created in different applications and pasted together into one big, compound document.

Using OLE to Create Compound Documents

Access includes an Edit Insert Object command that lets you add and create objects for a compound document.

If you want to know how to do this, refer to the **Embedding and Linking Objects** entry.

Distinguishing Between Linked Objects and Embedded Objects

A linked object—remember this might be a picture you've inserted into a field—gets updated whenever the source document changes. An embedded object doesn't. (You can, however, double-click an embedded object to open the application that created the embedded object to make your changes.)

What you absolutely need to know about OLE

Perhaps the most important tidbit for you to know about OLE is that it's very easy to use. You don't have to do anything other than copy and paste or insert the things—called objects—you want to plop into the compound document. If you're working with applications that support version 2.0 of OLE, you may also be able to drag-and-drop OLE objects between application windows.

Object Names Microsoft Access lets you name its database objects. To name the active database object—the object in the active document window—choose the File Save As command. Then, when Microsoft Access displays the Save As dialog box, enter a name. Your object name should be unique. Preferably it should be something clever. (Remember, it'll be this name that shows in the Database window whenever the database object's object button is selected.)

In naming an object—such as a table, a report, or a query—Access lets you use as many as 64 characters. You can use spaces, but you can't begin the name with a space. An object name can't contain a period, an exclamation point, brackets, or ASCII control characters.

 Database

ODBC ODBC is an abbreviation that stands for open database connectivity. The term usually refers to drivers—little control programs—that come with Access. These ODBC drivers let you connect Access to external **SQL** databases such as Microsoft SQL Server. You choose which ODBC drivers get installed when you set up Access.

Operators Microsoft Access provides mathematical and logical operators you can use in expressions for validation rules, for selection criteria, and for calculated fields.

Calculating values—**Mathematical Operators**
Comparing values and text—**Logical Operators**
Identifying people you maybe shouldn't trust—**Smooth Operators**

Outer-Join When Microsoft Access joins tables in a multiple-
table query, it typically runs something called an equi-
join. Basically, what this means is that you won't see
query results unless Access can successfully join records in
all the tables. For example, if you're joining customer
table records and customer order table records, Access
won't show customer order records for customers that
don't exist in the customer table. Usually, this is what you
want. If you don't care whether Access can successfully
join records in all the tables, you can run something
called an outer-join.

To create an outer-join, display the Query Design window for the query and double-click the join line. Or click
the join line and then choose the View Join Properties
command.

Mark either 2 or 3 to run
an outer-join.

☀ **Equi-Join; Joining Tables; Self-Join**

Passwords You can limit access to a database by adding a password. But be forewarned: This procedure is far more involved that you might guess if you're used to the way
passwords work in applications such as Lotus 1-2-3 or
WordPerfect. In Microsoft Access, passwords are only
one element of a rather sophisticated security system.

To assign passwords or use other elements of the Access
security system—for example, groups, user accounts, and
permissions—refer to the user documentation.

Primary Key The primary key is a **field** or combination of fields that uniquely identifies each **record** in a **table.** The primary key is also the **common field** in a primary table. You don't need to create primary keys for tables, but it's a good idea to do so. Primary keys improve performance and make it easier to define **relationships.**

You create a primary key as you design or redesign a table. You do this by selecting the field you want to use as the primary key and then choosing the Edit Set Primary Key command.

✦ **Foreign Key; Index**

Primary Table A primary table is what this book calls the main, or dominant **table,** in a table relationship. For example, in a database that holds customer information and customer orders information, your primary table will be the table that describes your customers. (The other table, the related table, will be the one that describes your customer orders.)

This primary table versus related table business sounds a bit funny at first. But let me make three observations that may help to clear up any confusion. The primary table in a **relationship** will probably be the one that you fill first. In the case of a customer and order database, for example, someone probably becomes a customer before or as you fill a customer order—not after.

The relationship between a primary table and a related table is often (although not always) a "one-to-many" relationship. In the case of a customer and orders database, each *one* customer table record will probably (hopefully?) tie to *many* customer order table records. (Other books call the primary table the "one" table for this reason.)

continues

Primary Table *(continued)*

Finally, a primary table often contains information that you use and would have to duplicate over and over in the related table. For example, if you put both customer and order information in the same table, you would enter much of the same customer information each time you processed an order: the customer name, the address, the shipping method, and so forth.

You can have more than one primary table in a database

You have a primary table in each table relationship. This means, of course, that if you have more than one table relationship in a database, you'll have more than one primary table. In fact, it's very possible that a table might be a related table in one relationship and a primary table in another relationship.

Primary Key

Printing
When you tell an application such as Microsoft Access to print a **document**—perhaps a **dynaset,** a **form,** or a **report**—what really happens is that the application creates a printable copy of the document (called a spool file in case you care) and then sends this printable copy to another application, Print Manager. Print Manager then prints the document.

Property
A property is simply a characteristic of a database object and of elements that constitute a database object. You can change the **field properties** of the **fields** in a **table,** for example. (A table is one example of a database object.)

QBE   Database folks seem to love abbreviations. This one stands for query-by-example. When you create a **query** in Microsoft Access, FYI, you are doing a QBE.

One other thing: The grid you see at the bottom of the Query Design window is called the QBE grid because it's where you enter the information that Access needs to perform the QBE.

Query   A query is fundamentally a question you ask Microsoft Access about data in a **table,** in a set of tables, or in another query. Let's say you've created a customer **database.** You might ask, "Who are my customers?" or "How many customers do I have?" Both questions are, in the parlance of databases, queries.

To query a database, you create a new database query object by doing three things. You tell Access which tables or queries you want to query. (You can query queries.) You tell Access which **fields** you want it to return as part of the answer. And you describe any manipulation—sorting or selection, for example—that should be performed as part and parcel of the query.

Identifying the Database and Tables

To identify the database and tables, follow these steps:

1 Open the database to which the query should be added.

2 Choose the Query object button.

3 Choose the New command button. Access displays the New Query dialog box, which, basically, asks whether you want to use a Query Wizard.

continues

Query *(continued)*

4 Assuming you're not interested in creating a **crosstabulation** query or one of the other special queries listed, choose the New Query command button. Access opens the Query design view window and displays the Add Table dialog box.

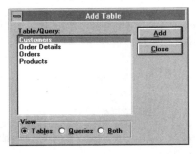

5 Select the table you'll query by clicking it and then choosing the Add command button.

6 Repeat step 5 for each table you want to query. You can also **query queries**; so if the data you want to ask a question about is in a query, mark the Queries button and then select the query.

7 Close the Add Table dialog box by choosing its Close command button. Access displays the Query design view window with boxes representing each of the to-be-queried tables or queries.

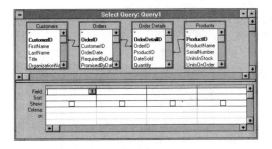

Joining Tables

If you want to combine, or join, tables in a query, the tables need to be connected by a **common field**, and you need to identify this common field either by setting up a **relationship** or by dragging the common field from the **primary table** to the common field in the related table. For example, if you're querying both a customer table and an orders table and both have the field "Customer ID," you've got a common field you can use to connect the tables. Access identifies a join by drawing a line between the common fields.

Choosing the Information the Query Returns

After you identify the tables you'll query, you tell Access which fields you want the query results to show. To do this, follow these steps:

1 Select the leftmost Field text box and activate its drop-down list box. (The drop-down list box arrow won't show until you select the field, in case you're wondering.)

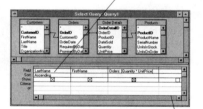

2 Select the first field that you want to see in the query results **dynaset,** that you want to use to sort, or that you want to use to select records. If you're querying multiple tables, Microsoft Access identifies both the table and the field names.

3 Repeat step 2 for each field you want.

4 This grid is called the QBE grid because it lets you query-by-example.

continues

Query *(continued)*

You can move and remove query fields

You can move a field and its column to a new location by selecting
it and then dragging it to a new location. You can remove a field
from the query by selecting it and then pressing Del or choosing the
Edit Delete command.

Running the Query

To run the query once you've told Access what you want to see,
choose the View Datasheet command. Or select the Datasheet View
tool.

Sorting the Query Results

To tell Access how it should sort the query results, follow these steps:

1 Select the field that Access should use first to alphabetize or order
the query results dynaset. For example, if you're querying an Access customer database, perhaps about year-to-date orders, you
might want to alphabetize the query results by customer name.

2 Activate the Sort drop-down list box for the field.

3 Select the sort order you want: Ascending, Descending, or not
sorted.

4 To use another field to sort query results with the same first, or
primary, sort field, repeat steps 1 through 3.

The trick to multiple-key sorting

The only trick to using a second key for sorting records
with the same first key is that the secondary sort key
must be in a column to the right of the first sort key.
Similiarly, if you want to use a third sort key for records
with the same first and second sort keys, the third sort
key must be in a column to the right of the second sort
key's column.

Specifying Selection Criteria for the Query

Use the Criteria and Or fields to specify whether you want the query to include or exclude information based on the contents of a field.

1 Select the field that Access should use first to select information for the query. If you're querying an Access customer database, perhaps about year-to-date international orders, you might want to exclude orders from domestic customers.

2 Enter the selection criteria for a field in the field's column. If you want find records with a field equal to a specific value, enter that value. If you want to find records with a text field holding a specific entry—such as the state equal to CA—enter that text. You can use **logical operators** to describe selection criteria.

Compound selection criteria

If you want to search for records with fields that meet all the selection criteria listed, enter the selection criterion into the same row of the QBE grid. If you want to search for records with fields that meet any one of the selection criteria, enter the selection criteria into separate rows of the QBE grid. You don't see the word "criterion" used much any more, do you? Me either.

continues

Query *(continued)*

Example Number-Field Selection Criteria

It isn't all that difficult to enter selection criteria into the Query window once you get the hang of it. But it can be a little tricky at first. So, with that admission, let me provide a few example selection criteria in a couple of tables. Here's a table that shows examples of number-field selection criteria:

Criterion	What it finds
5000	Finds records in which the field entry equals 5000
>5000	Finds records in which the field entry is greater than 5000
>5000 And <10000	Finds records in which the field entry is greater than 5000 and less than 10000
>=[Sales]*.75	Finds records in which the field entry is greater than or equal to 0.75, or 75%, of the value in the field named Sales. Entering this criterion for the field Cost of Goods, for example, finds records in which the Cost of Goods value is greater than or equal to 75% of the Sales value.
<1/1/95	Finds records in which the date field entry falls before January 1, 1995 (assuming this is the criterion for a Date/Time field)

Example Text-Field Selection Criteria

Text selection criteria work a bit differently. You can enclose the text in quotation marks. But if you don't include the quotation marks, Microsoft Access adds them for you. I've shown criteria that result in the same query results, by the way, to illustrate that there's often more than one way to skin a cat. The table on the next page shows examples of text-field selection criteria:

Criterion	What it finds
WA	Finds records in which the field entry is WA
"WA"	Finds records in which the field entry is WA
="WA"	Finds records in which the field entry is WA
W?	Finds records in which the field entry is two characters and starts with the letter W
Like ("W?")	Finds records in which the field entry matches this pattern: a two-character entry that starts with the letter W
W*	Finds records in which the field entry starts with the letter *W*. The field entry can be any length.
WA	Finds records in which the field entry uses the two-letter combination *WA* somewhere

Searching for embedded text in Memo and OLE object fields

You can use the asterisk character at the start and end of embedded text fragments that you want to search for in Memo fields and in embedded (but not linked) OLE Object fields.

Summary Calculations in a Query

To summarize the results of a query, construct the query in the usual way and select the Totals tool so that Access adds the Total row to the QBE grid. Then select the summary calculation that you want Access to make for a field.

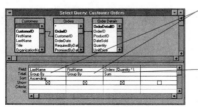

This tells Access that you want to group customer orders by customer names.

This tells Access that you want to sum orders. Orders get calculated as the quantity times the unit price. This is called a **calculated field.**

continues

Query *(continued)*

You can summarize the results of a query by calculating any of the following statistical measures for a field in the query result's dynaset:

Summary operator	What it does
Avg	Calculates the average of a field's nonblank entries
Count	Counts the number of nonblank field entries in the query result's dynaset
First	Returns the first record's field entry
Last	Returns the last record's field entry
Max	Finds the largest value in a field's nonblank entries in the query result's dynaset
Min	Finds the smallest value in a field's nonblank entries in the query result's dynaset
StDev	Calculates the standard deviation of nonblank field entries
Var	Calculates the variance of nonblank field entries
Sum	Calculates the total of a field's entries

You must summarize or group each field

If you choose to summarize the records that make up a query result, you must choose either the Group By operator or one of the summary operators described in the preceding table for each field in the QBE grid.

Reusing an Existing Query

To reuse a query—for example, when the database information changes—choose the Query object button and then double-click on the query. Access displays a datasheet view window with the query results information. If your query is complex or your database is large, Access may take a while to complete the query.

Redesigning a Query

You can change the design of a query. To perform these actions, choose the Query object button, select the query, and then choose the Design command button. Voila. Access displays the Query design view window. You make the changes you want and then close the window, saving your changes.

Printing Query Results

To print query results, choose the File Print command or select the Print tool. Note that **reports** provide a more elaborate way to get printed copies of the information in a dynaset.

Query Query

Query Query   A query query is a **query** of a query. In other words, it's a query in which you don't query a **table;** you query a query instead. Don't worry—you don't have to be able to say "query-query" three times fast. All you have to do to run one of these tongue twisters is select the query rather than the table as the **object** with data that you want to query.

RDBMS RDBMS is an abbreviation that stands for relational database management system. A relational database, such as Microsoft Access, stores its data in **tables.** Relational databases are all the rage nowadays. There are other types of databases, however—for example, the flat file databases one creates in spreadsheet programs like Microsoft Excel and Lotus 1-2-3.

Record Locks In a multiuser environment, Microsoft Access locks a **record** when it's being edited by a user. By locking the record, Access prevents some other user from simultaneously editing the record. How this record-locking business works is determined by the Multiuser/ODBC settings. You can change these settings by choosing the View Options command and selecting the Multiuser/ODBC category. There's quite a bit to record locks, however. So it might be a good idea to take a peek at the Microsoft Access user documentation.

 ODBC

Records A record is what gets stored in the rows of a **table.** It contains one or more **fields.**

Record Selectors Microsoft Access uses symbols or icons to convey useful information about the records in a **table.**

Symbol	What it means
🖉	Current record has been changed, but changes haven't been saved
✱	Empty row for the next record
▶	Current record that either hasn't been changed or whose changes have already been saved

Referential Integrity Referential integrity simply means that you can't enter a **record** in a related **table** unless the record ties, or connects, to a record in the **primary table.** OK. That sounds complicated. But let me give you an example. (You'll see what I mean right away.) Suppose you created a two-table database that tracks students and their course grades. In this situation, you might want to ensure that no course grade could be entered for a student who wasn't already described in the students table. To ensure this referential integrity, you close all objects and choose the Edit Relationships command, identify the Primary and Related Tables, identify their relationship, and mark the Enforce Referential Integrity check box.

:ʼ· **Relationships**

Relationships You can tell Microsoft Access how **tables** connect, or relate. For example, if you created a customer database, you might describe the relationship between customer table records and customer order table records. If you created a students database, you might describe the relationship between student table records and course grade table records.

continues

Relationships *(continued)*

Defining a Good Relationship

To describe the relationship between a **primary table** and any related tables, follow these steps:

1 Close all objects and choose the Edit Relationships command. Access, ever helpful, displays the Add Table dialog box if you haven't yet identified any relationships.

2 Select the tables for which you will define relationships by clicking and then choosing the Add command button.

3 Click the Close command button. Access removes the Add Table dialog box. You'll now see the Relationships window. Access shows any existing relationships by drawing a line from two tables' common **fields**.

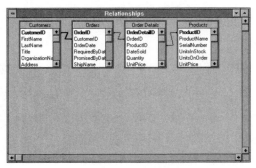

4 To define a relationship between two tables, drag the **common field** in the primary table to the common field in the related table.

5 To specify what type of relationship exists, double-click the relationship's line. Access displays the Relationships dialog box. (A bold line indicates a relationship for which Access enforces **referential integrity.**)

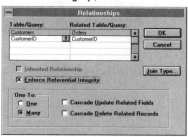

6 Mark the Enforce Referential Integrity check box if you think referential integrity is a good thing.

7 Use the One To option buttons to indicate how many records in the related table connect to a single record in the primary table. One indicates a one-record to one-record relationship; Many indicates a one-record to many-records relationship.

8 Choose OK.

Cascading referential integrity

The Cascade Update Related Fields and Cascade Delete Related Records check boxes relate to something called cascading referential integrity, which is a supercharged form of referential integrity. With cascading referential integrity, Access will delete and update records in related tables to maintain referential integrity.

Deleting a Relationship

To delete a relationship between two tables, select the relationship line and then press the Del key. You should be careful about deleting relationships, by the way. You may have other objects—queries, for example—that depend on the relationship.

ACCESS A TO Z

Renaming Database Files You use Microsoft Windows' File Manager to rename database files.

 Program Manager > **Main** > File Manager

Renaming a File

To rename a file once you've started File Manager, follow these steps:

1 Click the disk with the file.

2 Click the directory and, if necessary, the subdirectory that contains the file.

3 Select the file.

4 Choose the File Rename command.

5 Enter a new name for the file in the To text box.

6 Choose OK.

❧ Filenames

Renaming Objects To rename a database object, select the object in the database window. Then choose the File Rename command and enter a new name in the dialog box that Access provides.

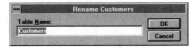

❧ Saving Databases and Objects

Replacing Record Fields

To find a specific **record** and replace the contents of one of its **fields,** display a **form** that shows the record or display the **datasheet** for the **table** that stores the record. Then choose the Edit Replace command.

1 In the Find What text box, specify what it is you're looking for.

2 In the Replace With text box, specify the replacement text.

3 Use the Search In option buttons to indicate whether Access should search only the current field or all the fields. (Searching only the current field is faster but your insertion point must be in the field you want to search.)

4 Use the Match Case check box to indicate whether Access should consider case (lower vs. upper) in its search. (Normally, Access ignores case.)

5 Use the Match Whole Field check box to indicate that Access should only find records if what you enter in the Find What text box matches a field's entire contents.

6 Choose Find Next to start and restart the search.

7 Choose Replace to replace the occurrence. Or choose Replace All to replace all the occurrences.

Wildcards

You can use wildcard characters in your Find What entry. The ? character can be used to represent any single character. The * character can be used to represent any single character or any combination of characters. The # character can be used to represent any digit combinations.

∴ **Finding Records; Wildcard Characters**

Reports Reports summarize the information in **tables** or **queries**.
A report is one of the three methods you have available
for viewing table data and query results. (The other two
methods are **forms** and **datasheets**.) Like a datasheet, a report shows multiple **records**. The difference is that you
can choose the format that a report uses to summarize
and show your table data. A datasheet, in comparison,
shows table data in a table.

Creating a Single Column Report

To create a report that lists only table records, follow these steps:

1 Open the **database** to which the report should be added. Access
displays the Database window.

2 Choose the Report object button.

3 Choose the New command button. Access displays the New Report dialog box.

4 Activate the drop-down list box and select the table or query you
want to create a report for.

5 Choose the Report Wizards command button. This tells Access
that you're busy and that you want it to do most of the the work of
setting up the report. Access displays the Report Wizards dialog
box, which asks which Microsoft Access Wizard you want to use.

6 Select Single-Column because you want only a list of the table records.

7 Choose OK. Access displays the first Single-Column Report Wizard dialog box.

8 Select the fields you want. You can select individual fields by clicking the field in the Available fields list box and then choosing the > button. You can select all the fields by choosing the >> button. You can remove a field from the Field order on report list box by clicking it and choosing <. You can remove all the fields from the Field order on report list box by choosing the << button.

9 Choose Next. Access displays another Single-Column Report Wizard dialog box. This one asks how you want your records sorted.

10 Select the first field you want Access to use for alphabetizing or arranging fields by clicking it in the Available fields list box and then choosing the > button. If needed, select another field to alphabetize or arrange records with the same first field in the same manner as you selected the first field. You can remove a field from the Sort order list box by clicking it and choosing <. If you want to start over, remove all the fields from the Sort order list box by choosing the << button.

continues

Reports *(continued)*

11 Choose Next. Access displays the third Single-Column Report Wizard dialog box. This one asks how you want your report to look.

12 Choose the option buttons that correspond to the "look" and orientation you want.

13 Choose Next. Access displays the next Single-Column Report Wizard dialog box, which asks what name it should use for the report object.

14 You can replace the suggested name if you want. When you're done, choose the Finish command button. Access displays your new report in a print preview window.

Creating a Summary Report

You can create a report that summarizes table records in a manner very similar to that used to create a single-column report. Follow these steps to do so:

1 Open the database to which the report should be added. Access displays the Database window.

2 Choose the Report object button.

3 Choose the New command button.

4 Activate the drop-down list box and select the table or query you want to create a report for.

5 Choose the Report Wizards command button.

6 Select Groups/Totals because you want to summarize records—for example, by counting records or totaling fields.

7 Choose OK. Microsoft Access displays the first Group/Totals Report Wizard dialog box.

8 Select the fields you want. You can select individual table fields by clicking the field in the Available fields list box and then choosing the > button. You can select all the table's fields by choosing the >> button. You can remove a field from the Field order on report list box by clicking it and choosing <. You can remove all the fields from the Field order on report list box by choosing the << button.

9 Choose Next. Access displays another Group/Totals Report Wizard dialog box. This one asks which fields should be used to group report rows into sets that will be summarized.

10 Select the fields you want to use to group: the first field first, the second field second, and the third field third, and so on. (Selecting more than one field lets you create groups within groups.)

continues

Reports *(continued)*

11 Choose Next. Access displays another Group/Totals Report Wizard dialog box. This one asks how to group data based on the Grouping field.

12 Select a grouping option. Select Normal to group records with the same value.

13 Choose Next. Access displays another Group/Totals Report Wizard dialog box.

14 Select the field you want Access to use for sorting.

15 Choose Next. Access displays another ReportWizard dialog box. This one will look familiar if you've produced a single-column report. It asks how you want your report to look.

16 Choose the option buttons that correspond to the "look" and orientation you want.

17 Choose Next. Access asks what name it should use for the report object. You can replace the suggested name if you want. When you're done, choose the Finish command button. Access displays your new report in a print preview window.

Previewing a Report

You can produce a report and preview it on your screen by opening the database, choosing the Report object button, and then double-clicking the report. When you do, Access displays a window that shows the printed pages of the report.

 Use the Zoom tools button to alternately magnify and then reduce the size of the page displayed in the Print Preview window.

If your report doesn't fit on the screen or on a single page, you can page through it using the horizontal and vertical scroll bars.

Printing a Report

To print a report, follow these steps:

1 Preview the report in the Print Preview window.

2 Choose the File Print command or select the Print tool. Access displays the Print dialog box.

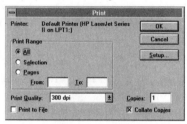

3 Use the Print Range options to print some portion of the report, for example pages 2-8.

4 Use the Print Quality drop-down list to specify a different output quality, or DPI resolution.

5 Use the Copies text box to print multiple copies of the report.

Closing a Report

When you finish reviewing the information in a report, close the report by double-clicking its Control-menu box. Or choose the File Close command.

If you haven't closed the report before, Access asks if you want to save it. If you indicate you do, Access presents a dialog box you can use to give the report object a descriptive name.

continues

Reports *(continued)*

Using an Existing Report

To use a report you already created, preview it as described earlier.

Redesigning a Report

You can change the design of a report manually. To do this, open the database with the report, choose the Report object button, double-click the report, and then choose the Design View tool. Access displays the Report design view window and the Report Design toolbox. You use these to modify the selected report.

Let me make an observation. Redesigning a report isn't terribly difficult, but it can be time-consuming. If you want to redesign a report, therefore, you may want to try creating a new report with the ReportWizard instead.

 **Mailing Labels**

Saving Databases and Objects If you've worked with other applications, you'll find that saving database objects to disk works a bit differently than you might expect.

Saving Changes to Records

If you add a record to a table or change the contents of some field, you'll want the addition or change saved. Because Access knows this, it saves your additions or changes automatically when you move to another record or when you tell Microsoft Access you want to add a new record. To sum things up then, you don't save changes to records; Access does. (All this also means you need to be careful: You may inadvertently do things that cause Access to save record changes you don't want to make.)

Saving Changes to an Object

You can save objects you create and save changes to existing objects' definitions. All you need to do is either choose the File Save As command (if you want to give the object a new name or if this is the first time you've saved the object) or choose the File Save command (if you want to use the existing name for an object you're changing). When you choose the File Save As command and haven't named the object before, Access displays a dialog box that asks, politely, for the object name.

Enter an object name here. Object names can be as many as 64 characters long.

☞ Back Up; Renaming Objects

Select Query A select query is a **query** that selects and sometimes summarizes **records.** The queries I describe in the
Query entry, for example, are all select queries. There are
other types of queries, however: **action queries,** for example, and crosstab queries.

☞ Crosstabulation

Self-Join A self-join is another type of table combination, or join.
It occurs when a table connects to itself. Why you would
do this is a bit suspicious, but it's just possible you will.
Refer to the Microsoft Access user documentation for
more information. (Sorry. With only 200 pages, I can't
cover everything the way they do in those huge tutorials
that do double-duty as a doorstop.)

☞ Joining Tables

Shortcut Menus A mostly cool new feature you're seeing in
many Windows-based applications, including Microsoft
Access, is the shortcut menu. Here's the scoop in case you
don't already know. Many applications are now smart
enough to know which commands make sense in which
situations. Many applications also know which commands you, as a user, are most likely to use in these situations. If you want them to, many applications will display
a menu of these commands—called the shortcut menu.
All you need to do is click the right button on the mouse.
(Remember that you use the left mouse button for selecting menus, commands, dialog box elements, and assorted
and sundry items.)

I haven't described the Access shortcuts menu commands
in this book because, although shortcut menus are fast,
they are more complicated to write about and read than
they are to use. See your Microsoft Access user documentation.

SQL SQL (pronounced "sequel") is another one of those database abbreviations. This one stands for Structured Query
Language. Basically, SQL is a database sublanguage (similar to a programming language) that databases understand and that you use (or that the database uses) to
retrieve data from the database.

 When you create a **query**, Access, ever the thoughtful
friend, actually creates the SQL statements that describe
your query. If you're interested in this, you can see what
the SQL statements look like by choosing the View SQL
command when you've displayed the Query object window or by selecting the SQL View tool.

Connecting to a SQL database?

If you're planning to use Microsoft Access to connect to a SQL data-base, you will need to have installed the appropriate ODBC driver when you installed Microsoft Access.

 ODBC

Starting Microsoft Access
You start Microsoft Access— and all Windows-based applications—either manually after you've started Windows or as part of starting Windows.

Starting Microsoft Access Manually

To start Microsoft Access manually, follow these steps:

1 Start Windows—for example, by typing *win* at the MS-DOS prompt.

2 Display the program group in which Access is an item. For example, if the Microsoft Access program group is Microsoft Office (which it probably is), choose the Window Microsoft Office command from the Program Manager menu bar.

3 Double-click the Microsoft Access program item.

Starting Microsoft Access Automatically

To start Microsoft Access each time Windows starts, follow these steps:

1 Start Windows—for example, by typing *win* at the MS-DOS prompt.

2 Display the program group in which Access is an item. For ex-ample, if the Access program group is Microsoft Office, choose the Window Microsoft Office command from the Program Manager menu bar.

3 Display the StartUp program group—for example, by choosing the Window StartUp command from the Program Manager menu bar.

4 Drag the Microsoft Access program item from the program group window—such as Microsoft Office—to the StartUp program group window to move the program item. Or, if you just want to duplicate the program item, hold down Ctrl while you drag.

continues

Starting Microsoft Access *(continued)*

StartUp program groups

The StartUp group is a program group of applications that start automatically whenever you start Windows. This is why you copy or move the Microsoft Access program item to the StartUp group if you want to automatically start Microsoft Access.

Subform

A subform is a **form** that's attached to another form. You typically create a subform when you want to show related records from two objects. The form to which this new subform is attached is called a main form.

If you base the main form and the subform on **tables,** the main form will probably show a **primary table,** and the subform will show the related table. The **relationship** between the main form table and the subform table will be one-to-many.

Creating a Form That Uses a Subform

To attach a subform to a main form, follow these steps:

1 Open the **database** to which the form should be added. Access displays the Database window.

2 Choose the Form object button.

3 Choose the New command button. Access displays the New Form dialog box.

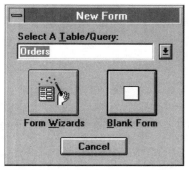

4 Activate the Select a Table/Query drop-down list box and select the object upon which the main form should be based.

5 Choose the Form Wizards command button. This tells Access that you want it to go to most of the the work of setting up the form. Access displays the Form Wizards dialog box, which asks which Wizard you want to use.

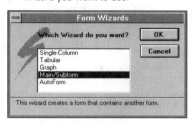

6 Choose Main/Subform to create a form that uses a subform. Access displays the first Main/Subform Wizard dialog box.

7 Indicate upon which table or **query** the subform should be based by selecting the object from the list box. You can use the View option buttons that appear beneath the list box to select which types of objects should be listed: tables, queries, or both.

8 Choose Next. Access displays the next Main/Subform Wizard dialog box that asks which **fields** should appear on the main form.

9 Select the fields you want in the order they should appear on the main form. You can select individual table fields by clicking the field in the Available fields list box and then choosing the > button. You can select all the table's fields by choosing the >> button. You can remove a field from the Field on main form list box by clicking it and choosing <. You can remove all the fields from the Field on main form list box by choosing the << button.

continues

Subform *(continued)*

10 Choose Next. Access displays the next Main/Subform Wizard dialog box, which asks which fields should appear on the subform.

11 Select the fields you want in the order they should appear on the subform. Selecting fields for the subform works the same way as selecting fields for the main form, which is described in step 9.

12 Choose Next. Access displays another Main/Subform Wizard dialog box. This one asks how you want your form to look.

13 Choose the option buttons that correspond to the "look" you want.

14 Choose Next. Access displays yet another Main/Subform Wizard dialog box. This one asks what name Access should use for the main form and whether you want to start using the form or want instead to redesign some of the form by fiddling with its **control objects.** You can replace the suggested name if you want. But you probably needn't worry about redesigning the form—especially if you're in a hurry.

15 Choose Finish. Access displays a message that says you must save the subform. Choose OK and then give the subform an object name.

16 When you're done, choose the OK command button. Access displays your new form.

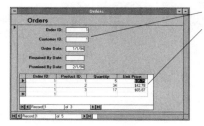

This is the main form.

This is the subform.

Switching Tasks To multitask, or run multiple applications, in the Windows operating environment, you use the Control menu's Switch To command. Choosing this command displays the Task List dialog box, which works as described below:

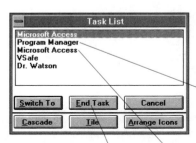

The Task List dialog box lists Program Manager as well as any other applications you or Windows has started.

To start a new application, double-click Program Manager. Then, when Windows displays Program Manager, use it to start another application.

To switch to an application already running, double-click it. Or select it with the direction keys or the mouse, and choose Switch To.

Use the Cascade, Tile, and Arrange Icons command buttons to manage the application windows of the applications you've started.

You can use the End Task command button to stop a Windows-based application.

Easy switching

You can cycle through the applications listed in the Task List dialog box using the keyboard. Press Alt+Tab to return to the last active application. Or hold down the Alt key and repeatedly press Tab to see message boxes that list the running applications, and release the Alt and Tab keys when the message box names the application you want to switch to. You can also press Alt+Esc to move through the open applications.

Tables A table is the container that a relational database such as Microsoft Access uses for holding data. Each table stores **records** with the same **fields.**

This grid is called a **datasheet.**

Each record goes into its own row.

Each field goes in its own column.

Creating Your First Table with the Table Wizard

To create a table with the Table Wizard, follow these steps:

1 Open the database to which the table should be added. Or create the database if it doesn't yet exist.

2 Choose the Table object button.

3 Choose the New command button. Access displays the New Table dialog box.

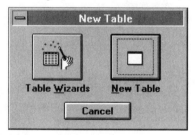

4 Choose the Table Wizards command button. Access displays the first Table Wizard dialog box.

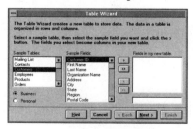

5 Choose the Business or Personal button to tell Access which list of sample tables it should display.

continues

115

Tables *(continued)*

6 Select an entry from the Sample Tables list. If you were building a customers table, for example, you would select the Customers entry.

7 Select the fields you want. You can select individual table fields by clicking the field in the Sample Fields list box and then choosing the > button. You can select all the table's fields by choosing the >> button. You can remove a field from the Fields in my new table list box by clicking it and choosing <. You can remove all the fields from the Fields in my new table list box by choosing the << button.

8 Choose Next. Access displays another Table Wizard dialog box. This one asks you to name the table and whether Access should specify the **primary key.**

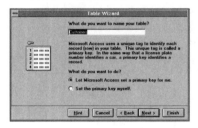

9 Name the table.

10 Select the option button that indicates Microsoft Access should set the primary key for you. (If you don't have an appropriate primary key field in your table, Access will add a **counter** field and use it as the primary key.)

11 Choose Finish. Access displays yet another Table Wizard dialog box. This one asks if you want to modify the table design, add records using a **datasheet,** or add records using a **form** that Access will create for you.

12 Indicate whether you want to modify the table design or add records and then choose Finish.

Creating Subsequent Tables with the Table Wizard

Creating a second table with the Table Wizard works in a manner very similar to creating your first table. The only difference in creating a subsequent table with the Table Wizard is that Access asks how the new table is related to existing tables. (This occurs after step 10 described in the preceding set of steps.)

This list box describes Access's best guess as to how the new table relates to existing tables. If a **relationship** is incorrect, select the relationship and then choose the Change command button. Access displays a dialog box you use to change the relationship.

Creating a Table from Scratch

To create a table, follow these steps:

1 Open the database to which the table should be added. Or create the database if it doesn't yet exist.

2 Choose the Table object button.

3 Choose the New command button. Access displays the New Table dialog box.

4 Choose the New Table command button. Access displays the table's design view in a window.

5 Enter a name for each of the table's fields in the Field Name column.

6 Activate the Data Type drop-down list and select a **data type**.

continues

Tables *(continued)*

7　Describe the field using the Description text box. (Access displays this description in the status bar whenever the field is selected in a datasheet or form.)

8　Repeat steps 5 through 7 for each of the table's fields.

9　Select a **primary key** field; then choose the Edit Set Primary Key command.

10　Close the Table design view window—for example, by double-clicking its Control-menu box.

11　When Access asks, give the table an **object name**.

Filling a Table with a Datasheet View Window

To fill the table with data, you can use a **datasheet.** To do this, choose the View Datasheet command. If Access asks about saving the changes to your table, go ahead and give the "thumbs-up" signal by choosing OK.

Note that you can also use a form to fill a table with data.

Copying data

You can copy the previous record's field contents into the same field in the current record by pressing Ctrl+'. In other words, you press the Ctrl key and the apostrophe key.

Editing Data in a Table's Datasheet

To edit the data in a table's datasheet, simply click the field to select its contents. Erase the selected field's contents by pressing Del. Or replace the selected field's contents by typing. Insert stuff by repositioning the insertion point using the Left and Right direction keys and then typing. (Access inserts whatever you type at the insertion point.) Use the Backspace key to erase the character preceding the insertion point.

Opening an Existing Table

To view an existing table's information in a **datasheet window**, open the database, choose the Table object button, and then double-click the table. Access displays a datasheet window with the table information.

Redesigning a Table

You can change the design of a table by adding and removing columns, or fields. To do this, choose the Table object button, select the table, and then choose the Design command button. Voilà. Microsoft Access displays the table window. It uses rows to describe each field in the table.

To delete a column, or a field, from a table, select the row that describes the column and then choose the Edit Delete Row command or press Del.

To insert a field in the table, select the field in front of which the field should be inserted. Then choose the Edit Insert Row command and fill in the blank row that Access inserts.

Changing field properties

You can change field properties, but you need to be careful. Very careful indeed. If you reduce a field's field size from 50 characters to 10, for example, any original field entries longer than 10 charac-ters will get cut off. If you change a field's data type, you may lose data if part of the original field entry won't fit in the new data type. You also need to be careful when you start fooling around with things like primary keys and indexes. If you create a "No duplicates" index and there are duplicate field entries in the table, Access will remove the duplicate entries. Yikes. I should mention that Access won't make a table design change that leads to data loss without asking you if you're aware of the possible data loss.

Printing a Table

To print a table's information, first open it. Then choose the File Print command or select the Print tool. Note that Microsoft Access's's **Reports** provide a more elaborate way to get printed copies of the information in a table.

Closing a Table

When you finish entering or editing table data, close the table by double-clicking its Control-menu box. Or choose the File Close command. Access, ever the thoughtful friend, returns you to the Database window.

Field Properties; Importing Data; Printing

Table Wizard The Table Wizard creates **tables** almost automatically. All you do is answer a handful of simple questions presented on some dialog boxes. For more information, refer to the preceding entry.

Toolbox If you view a **report** or **form** object in the design **view,** you'll see something called the toolbox. The toolbox provides a series of command buttons you can click to add **control objects** to forms and reports. Here's a list of the tools and what they do. If you have questions, your best bet is probably to use the **Control Wizards.** It will step you through adding or modifying control objects.

Icon	Description
	Selects a control object so that you can move and resize it
	Adds a label
	Adds a text box
	Groups a set of options control objects—for example, option buttons
	Adds a command button that you can select and deselect. If selected, the command button appears depressed.
	Adds an option button
	Adds a check box
	Adds a combo box
	Adds a list box
	Adds a graph
	Adds a **subform** to a **form** or **report** or embeds a report in another existing report
	Adds a picture, a **graph,** or an OLE object that isn't stored in a **table**

	Adds a picture, a graph, or an OLE object that is stored in a table
	Adds a line
	Adds a rectangle
	Adds a page break
	Adds a command button such as you might use for a **macro button**
	Turns on and off the Control Wizards
	Tells Microsoft Access to keep the selected tool active until you select a different tool

Toolbox button names

If you place the mouse over a toolbox button, Access displays the tool name in a tiny yellow box.

Undo   You can undo your changes to a **record** or a **field**. To reverse the changes you've just made to a field if you haven't yet selected a new field, choose the Edit Undo Typing command or select the Undo tool.

 To reverse all the changes you've made to a field, choose the Edit Undo Current Field command.

To reverse all the changes you've made to the current record or the record you last changed, choose either the Edit Undo Current Record command or the Edit Undo Saved Record command. I'll let you guess which command does what, OK?

Validation Rules

A validation rule is an **expression** that Microsoft Access uses to evaluate an entry that you or someone attempts to place in a **field.** If what gets entered into the field matches the expression, Access allows the entry. If what gets entered into the field doesn't match the expression, Access doesn't allow the entry.

One other thing: Access validates only field entries. So, if nothing gets entered into a field, Access doesn't do any validation.

Validation Comparison Operators

Validation rules use **logical operators.**

Operator	Valid field entries must be
=	Equal to what follows the operator. For example, the validation rule =100 means that the field entry must equal 100. And ="CA" means that the field entry must be the two characters CA.
>=	Greater than or equal to what follows the operator. For example, the validation rule >=100 means the field entry must be greater than or equal to 100.
>	Greater than what follows the operator. For example, the validation rule >100 means that the field entry must be greater than 100.
<=	Less than or equal to what follows the operator. For example, the validation rule <=100 means that the field entry must be less than or equal to 100.
<	Less than what follows the operator. For example, the validation rule <100 means that the field entry must be less than 100.
<>	Not equal to what follows the operator. For example, the validation rule <>100 means that the field entry must not equal 100.
And	Meet two validation rules. For example, the validation rule >=100AND<1000 means that the field entry must be greater than or equal to 100 and less than 1000.

V

Operator	Valid field entries must be
Or	Meet one of the validation rules described. For example, the validation rule ="CO"OR="WA" means that the field entry must either be the two characters CO or the two characters WA.
Like	Composed of specified characters. For example, the validation rule Like "??" means the field entry can use only two characters. And the validation rule Like "###" means the field entry can use only three numbers.

 **Field Properties**

Validation rules ignore case

Validation rules ignore case (upper vs. lower). So, the validation rule ="CA" allows the field entries CA, ca, cA, and Ca.

Views

You can look at database **objects** from more than a single perspective: You can look at **tables** and **reports,** for example, from either a design view or a datasheet view. You can look at **forms** from a design view, a datasheet view, or a form view. And you can look at **queries** from a design view, from a **SQL** view, or from a datasheet view.

Datasheet and Form Views

One way of looking at a database object is by looking at the actual data that the object stores or retrieves. If the data from a table or query appears in a **datasheet,** for example, this view is called the datasheet view of the table or query. That makes sense, right?

If the data for a form appears in a form, this view is called the form view of the form. This last bit of information seems confusing, but you can also view the data for a form in a datasheet, which as you know now, is called the datasheet view of the form.

continues

Views *(continued)*

Design View

Another way of looking at an object is by looking at the description of the object. This is called the design view. When you're creating a table by describing its **fields,** for example, you'll be looking not at the table's data but at the table's design.

SQL View

The SQL view of a query object shows the SQL statements that describe a query.

Flip-Flopping between Views

 You can look at a database object's design view in a window by selecting the Design View tool.

 You can look at a database object's data view in a **datasheet window** by selecting the Datasheet View tool.

 You can look at a database object's data view in a form window if a form has been designed by selecting the Form View tool.

 You can look at a query object's SQL view in a window by selecting the SQL View tool.

Wildcard Characters

Wildcard characters are characters that can stand for other characters in an **expression.** The most common wildcard characters are the ? and * symbols. A ? can stand for any single character. An * can stand for any single character or any group of characters. Access also supplies a # wildcard character that can stand for any single digit.

You can indicate that you're looking for specific characters by including the characters in brackets, [and]. For example, the entry *N[ie]lson* would find both *Nelson* and *Nilson.*

You can specify that you don't want to find the letters inside the brackets by preceding the characters with an exclamation point. For example, the entry N[!e]lson would find any five-letter entry that started with an *N* and ended with *lson* except *Nelson.*

You can also specify that you want to find a range of letters inside the brackets by using the hyphen. For example, the entry *N[a-e]lson* would find entries such as *Nalson* and *Nelson* but not *Nilson* or *Nolson*.

If you're interested in this whole wildcard thing, take a peek at the **Validation Rules** entry and at the **Query** entry. They both show more examples of wildcard usage.

Wild Characters Wild characters are simply house guests that arrive unannounced, open bags of potato chips without asking, and then drink all the beer in your refrigerator. Don't confuse these unsavory folks with the useful-but-similarly-entitled tool, **Wildcard Characters.**

Wizards Microsoft Access Wizards help you create database **objects.** There are Wizards to assist you in the creation of **tables, forms,** and **reports,** for example. Because this is a quick-help book, I almost always describe how to accomplish a task by using a Microsoft Access Wizard.

TROUBLE-SHOOTING

Got a problem? Starting on the next page are solutions to the problems that plague new users of Microsoft Access. You'll be on your way—and safely out of danger—in no time.

DATA ENTRY

You Get a Duplicate Key Error

If you get a duplicate key error, it means that you've entered the same value for a **primary key** field for the record as some other, existing record uses. Yet the primary key value can't be duplicated. This contradiction, in effect, triggers the error.

Use a different primary key value

Because there shouldn't be duplicated primary key values, you simply need to use a different primary key for the new record you're trying to add. That's all there is to it.

You Can't Enter a Calculated Field for a Table

The problem here is that **tables** store only raw data. You don't use them to calculate numbers or to store the results of calculations. It may just be, though, that you do want a calculation made. For example, a table that stores the quantities and unit prices of products ordered by a customer should logically calculate the order amount by multiplying the quantity by the unit price, right? Shoot. If it doesn't and you want to know the order amount, you'll have to make the calculation yourself.

Create a query that uses the calculated field

You can create a **query** that makes the calculation you want in a calculated field. Note that you can use a query object to provide data to **forms,** to **reports,** and even to other queries. So, for all practical purposes, you can think of a query as a table.

You Can't Change a Locked Record

This book does not talk much about using Access in a multiuser environment. But if you are, I need to tell you about the effect of something called record locking. You can't change a record that some other user is editing if record locking is turned on. This makes sense if you think about it. If both you and the guy in the next cubicle make changes to a record, Access doesn't know how to reconcile the changes when you guys try to save them.

Wait a while and try again

Your best bet is to wait a bit and see if Access unlocks the record when whoever is editing it finishes up. Once the record is unlocked, you'll be able to see it and make whatever changes you want.

Editing etiquette

Because you lock records when you edit them, thereby preventing others from accessing them, minimize the time you spend editing a record. You don't, for example, want to display some record in a form, ponder possible changes for 20 minutes, and then head off for a 2-hour lunch with the form still showing the record on your screen. At least you don't want to do this if you work with people you like.

You Can't Sort Table Records

Microsoft Access doesn't sort table **records** as you enter them. This can seem funny. Logically, it seems as if Access should instantly organize them some other way—perhaps based on the **primary key** or **index,** for example. But, alas, it doesn't.

Use the Quick Sort commands

To sort a table's records in ascending order based on some **field,** select the field and then choose the Records Quick Sort Ascending command.

To sort a table's records in descending order based on some field, select the field and then choose the Records Quick Sort Descending command.

Create a query

To sort a table's records in some more complicated order—such as based on several key fields—simply create a select **query.**

Let me point out a useful ort of information. You can use a query **object** in all the same ways you use a table object. You can create **reports** that use query objects, for example. And you can create **forms** that you can use to fill a query object's **dynaset** (and, therefore, the queried tables) with data.

An "ort," by the way, is simply a fragment, bit, or scrap—such as an ort of food. I use the word here for two reasons. One is that "ort" is a cool word. Second is that I want to give you a leg up on the competition the next time you play Scrabble.

QUERY

You Want to Search for Text that Uses an Operator

If you want to search for a text string that includes an **operator** such as "and" or "or," you can't just enter the text string into the selection criteria row.

Enclose the text string in quotation marks

To search for a text string that uses a word that Microsoft Access also uses as an operator, enclose the text string in quotation marks.

Field:	Title
Sort:	
Show:	☒
Criteria:	"Rock and roll"
or:	

To search for the phrase *Rock and roll,* for example, you need to enter this string in quotation marks as shown here.

Field:	Title
Sort:	
Show:	☒
Criteria:	"Rock" And "roll"
or:	

If you don't enclose the text string in quotation marks, Access assumes that the word that looks like an operator is an operator. In this case, for example, Access encloses the words "Rock" and "roll' in quotation marks because it assumes you're looking for records with Title fields equal to "Rock" and "roll." No single field can contain two separate entries, so this selection criteria never selects a record.

 Query

Your OR Works Like an AND

When you use more than a single criterion to select records in a **query,** it's easy to have criteria you mean to have applied individually instead be applied collectively. The key thing to remember is that each row of selection criteria information in a **QBE** describes a set of selection criteria that must all be met in order for records to be selected.

Field:	Last Name	Birth Date
Sort:		
Show:	☒	☒
Criteria:	Like "B" Or Like "C"	>#1/1/60#
or:		

For a record to be selected in this query, the last name must start with the letter "B" or "C," and the birth date must fall after January 1, 1960. A record for someone with the last name Nelson and a birthday in 1959 won't get selected, for example. Neither will a record for someone with the last name Baker and a birthday in 1969.

Field:	Last Name	Birth Date
Sort:		
Show:	☒	☒
Criteria:	Like "B" Or Like "C"	
or:		>#1/1/60#

For a record to be selected in this query, either the last name must start with the letter "B" or "C" or the birth date must fall after January 1, 1960. A record for someone with the last name Nelson and a birthday in 1959 will get selected, for example, because of the birthday. And a record for someone with the last name Baker and a birthday in 1969 will get selected because of the last name.

FILES

You Can't Save a Database

Microsoft Access needs a certain amount of system resources, or memory, to save a database file. If your system resources get too low, therefore, you can run into a pretty serious problem: You may not be able to save your database. Fortunately, as long as you keep your cool, this doesn't have to be a disaster. Your basic tack is a simple one. You want to free up system resources and then try resaving the database.

Close your other open applications

Switch to any of your other open applications and close them. You can switch to the other open applications by choosing the Microsoft Access Control menu's Switch To command, selecting the other application from the Task List dialog box, and then choosing the End Task command button.

Once you've closed all the other applications (and saved their documents if that's appropriate), return to Access and try resaving the database you couldn't earlier save.

If you're the superstitious sort, go ahead and cross your fingers. It won't make any difference. But it may make you feel better.

Saving Databases and Objects; Switching Tasks

You Accidentally Erased a Database

If you've just erased a database file—for example, by using File Manager's File Delete command or the MS-DOS Del command—stop what you're doing. Don't save anything else to your hard disk. It may be possible to recover, or unerase, a database file.

Use the MS-DOS Undelete command

How you unerase files is beyond the scope of this little book: The mechanics really relate to MS-DOS and not to Access. So you'll need to look up the File Undelete command in your MS-DOS user documentation.

I will say this. When MS-DOS deletes a file, it doesn't actually erase the disk file. Instead, it simply adds the database's disk space to its list of locations that can now be used to store new data. Eventually, the database file data will be overwritten with some new file. But, if you haven't yet saved a new file over the database's old disk location, the database file still exists. In this case, you can undelete the file.

 Database; Saving Databases and Objects

You Can't Remember Your Password

If you or someone else assigned a password to a database file using the Security Change Password command, you'll need to supply that password whenever you start Microsoft Access. If you forget your password or can't seem to enter it correctly, Access won't start.

Try a password with different-case letters

Access differentiates passwords on the basis of the letter case. The following words, for example, are all different passwords from Microsoft Access's point of view: Wathers, wATHERS, and WATHERS. For this reason, if you think you know the password, try changing all the lowercase letters to uppercase letters and vice versa. It may be that you entered the password with a different combination of upper- and lower case letters than you think. (This can happen, for instance, if you happened to press the Caps Lock key before entering the password.)

Get help from the database administrator

If you've tried the technique described in the preceding paragraph and still can't enter your password, you need help. For this help, see the database administrator. This person will probably be the same guy or gal who originally provided your password and user name.

 Database; Saving Databases and Objects

Your Hard Disk Is Full

If your hard disk begins to fill up, you'll either want to free up some space or buy a bigger disk. Presumably, the database you're maintaining with Microsoft Access will grow over time.

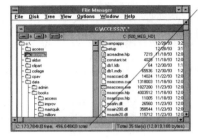

Check your free disk space by starting File Manager, selecting the hard disk's root directory, and then reading the status bar on the bottom, left side of the window.

Erase any unneeded files

The most direct way to free up disk space is to remove individual files from the disk using File Manager's File Delete command. If you want to save the files, you can first copy them to a floppy disk.

I feel stupid saying this, but in general it's not a good idea to remove files you didn't create in the first place. It may be, for example, that you and Microsoft Windows or you and some application (such as Access, for example) have different ideas as to whether a file is needed.

If you're the adventurous sort

One possible exception that I feel uncomfortable even bringing up concerns files with the extension TMP. The TMP extension usually means that a file is temporary. And temporary usually means "not permanent" and "of passing importance." So, usually, you can erase files with the TMP extension without much risk. This is especially true if the last modification date of the file shows the file hasn't been used for a long time. *Please, please, please* don't do this without thoroughly checking the user documentation for the application that created the TMP files. Who knows? Maybe some geek has decided that TMP no longer means "temporary."

Use Windows Setup to remove extra baggage

You can use the Windows Setup application to remove programs (such as the Windows accessories you don't need), Readme files you don't read, and some of the little extra stuff that hangs around on disk and consumes space (such as the bit map images). If you already know how to do this, great. If you don't, refer to the Microsoft Windows user documentation.

Use disk compression

MS-DOS version 6 and later comes with a disk compression utility, DoubleSpace. You may want to use DoubleSpace to scrunch more data on your disk. For more information on DoubleSpace, refer to the MS-DOS user documentation.

Change the way UNDELETE works

How you use the Undelete command that comes with MS-DOS version 5 and later can dramatically affect how quickly you fill up your hard disk. Here's why: You can tell the Undelete command to use its Delete Sentry option, in which case it makes a copy of files you delete just in case you later want to undelete one.

You may want to check the Undelete options you've chosen. If you're using the Delete Sentry option, weigh the extra security it provides (in terms of recovering deleted files) with the high cost in hard disk usage.

For more information on Undelete, refer to the MS-DOS user documentation.

You Can't Save a File to a Floppy Disk

If you attempt to save a database file or copy a database file to a floppy disk but can't, there are several things you can try.

Unprotect the floppy disk

If you get a message that says a disk is write-protected, you won't be able to save a database file, or write, to the disk until you unprotect the disk.

To write to a 5.25-inch floppy disk, verify that the floppy disk has a notch. If a piece of tape or an adhesive tab is covering up this notch, you won't be able to write anything to the disk. To unprotect the floppy disk, remove the tape or adhesive tab covering the notch.

To write to a 3.5-inch floppy disk, verify that there is no square hole in the disk's top right corner when you're holding the disk so you can read its label. If there is a square hole, flip the floppy disk over, and move the slide that covers the hole.

Why the write-protection

I don't mean to sound like a worrier, but before you decide it's OK to write to a previously write-protected floppy disk, you may want to consider the reasons someone protected the disk. Who knows? Maybe there's stuff on the disk that shouldn't be written over.

Format the floppy if needed

If you get a message that Windows or a Windows-based application such as File Manager can't read a disk, it may be because the disk isn't formatted. If you know this is the case or you know there's nothing on the floppy disk that you or the person in the next cubicle needs, you can format the floppy disk. (For practical purposes, formatting a disk destroys everything that's on it.) Refer to either the Microsoft Windows or the MS-DOS user documentation for information on how to do this.

Verify there's room

A floppy disk doesn't have all that much room compared with a hard disk. It's quite likely that your database file will soon grow too large to fit on a single floppy disk. In this event, you'll need to back up the database file to multiple floppy disks or to a tape if you want to make a separate copy of the database.

WINDOWS AND APPLICATIONS

You've Started More Than One Copy of Microsoft Access

If you begin multitasking with the Control menu's Switch To command, it's not all that difficult to find you've started multiple copies of an application—including Access. This unnecessarily consumes memory. And it makes it difficult to share data across applications.

Exit from the active Access application

If one of the Access application tasks is active—meaning the Access application window shows on your screen—you can exit from it. (Do this with the File Exit command.) This closes the active Access task, but the other inactive Access task will still be open, or running.

Close the second Access task

If another application or Program Manager is active, follow these steps to close the second, extra Access task:

1 Choose the application's Control menu's Switch To command—for example, by pressing Ctrl+Esc.

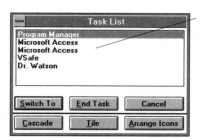

2 Select one of the Access applications from the task list—for example, by double-clicking.

3 When the Access application window appears, choose the File Exit command.

 Control-menu Commands; Switching Tasks

You Want to Cancel a Printing Document

If you've told Access to print a report you later realize you don't want to print, you may want to cancel the printing. This is particularly true if the report is long and you'd really prefer not to waste the paper.

Press Esc if Access shows a "Printing" message box

If Access shows a message box on your screen that says something along the lines of "Printing Document," you can cancel the printing by pressing Esc or by clicking the message box's Cancel command button.

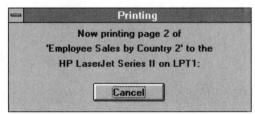

Printing

Now printing page 2 of
'Employee Sales by Country 2' to the
HP LaserJet Series II on LPT1:

Cancel

continues

You Want to Cancel a Printing Document *(continued)*

Switch to Print Manager and delete the job

When Access prints a document—a report, say—it creates a print spool file that it sends to the Windows Print Manager. Print Manager then prints this print spool file as well as any other spool files that Access and other applications have sent.

To cancel printing an Access document once it's been sent to Print Manager, you need to follow these steps:

1 Choose the Access Control menu's Switch To command—for example, by pressing Ctrl+Esc.

2 Select the Print Manager application from the task list—for example, by double-clicking.

3 Click the printing Access document.

4 Choose Print Manager's Delete command button.

⁘ Control-menu Commands; Printing; Switching Tasks

You Can't Get Access to Respond

It's unlikely but still possible that a bug in Microsoft Access will cause it to stop responding. If this happens, you won't be able to choose menu commands. And you may not be able to move the mouse pointer.

Terminate the unresponsive application

Unfortunately, if an application truly is unresponsive—if it ignores your keyboard and mouse actions—there's nothing you can do to make it start responding again. When this is the case, however, you can press Ctrl+Alt+Del.

Ctrl+Alt+Del—you press the three keys simultaneously—tells Windows to look at the active application and check for responsiveness. Windows makes this check and displays a message that tells you whether the application is, in fact, unresponsive.

```
This Windows application has stopped responding to the system.

*  Press ESC to cancel and return to Windows.
*  Press ENTER to close this application that is not responding.
*  You will lose any unsaved information in this application.
*  Press CTRL+ALT+DELETE to restart your computer. You will
   lose any unsaved information in all applications.

      Press ENTER for OK or ESC to cancel: OK
```

As the message text indicates, you can simply press Enter to close the unresponsive application. By the way, if the application isn't unresponsive, Windows knows this, and the message text indicates as much. In this case, you can press Enter to return to the application.

continues

You Can't Get Access to Respond *(continued)*

Patience is a virtue

Before you conclude that Microsoft Access or some other application is ignoring you, consider the possibility that it is busy instead. Access, for example, may be running a macro or an Access Basic module. Other applications may be printing to a spool file (which gets sent to Print Manager for printing) or may be executing some command you've given.

You Get an Application Error

Sometimes an application asks Windows to do the impossible. When this happens— which isn't very often since the advent of Windows version 3.1, thankfully—Windows displays a message box that says there's been an application error.

Close the application

When Windows does alert you to an application error, it usually gives you two choices. You can close the application, or you can ignore the error.

If you've been working with a database and have made changes that you haven't yet saved, you can ignore the application error and then save the document. Save the database using a new filename, however. You don't want to replace the previous database file with a new corrupted database file. Then close the Access application.

If you haven't made any changes or haven't made changes you need to save, simply close the application.

QUICK REFERENCE

Any time you explore some exotic location, you're bound to see flora and fauna you can't identify. To make sure you can identify the commands and toolbar buttons you see in Microsoft Access, the Quick Reference describes these items in systematic detail.

STARTUP WINDOW MENU GUIDE

File Menu

New Database...	Creates a new, empty database. You specify the name of the database file and its location.
Open Database...	Retrieves an existing database from disk
Compact Database...	Rearranges a database file so that it isn't fragmented and so that it takes less disk space
Convert Database...	Does some fancy stuff with a Microsoft Access version 1.x database file so that it can be opened with Microsoft Access version 2.0
Encrypt/Decrypt Database...	Jumbles and unjumbles the characters in a database file so that the file can't be read by other programs—such as a word processor
Repair Database...	Patches up a corrupted database so that you can use it again
Toolbars...	Adds and removes toolbars from the application window
Unhide	Unhides previously hidden windows
Run Macro...	Starts a macro program
Add-ins	Displays the Add-ins submenu
Add-in Manager	Adds and removes Add-in utilities such as the Query Wizard and the Form and Report Wizards
Database Documentor	Produces reports that describe database objects
Attachment Manager	Attaches non–Access tables to an Access database
Import Database...	Lets you import a database created by another database application
Menu Builder	Lets you build and modify custom menus
Exit	Closes, or stops, the Access application

Help Menu

Contents	Lists the major Help topic categories
Search...	Provides help on a topic you specify
Cue Cards	Turns on Microsoft Access Cue Cards, which coach you through the steps for database management tasks
Technical Support	Tells about support available for Access
About Microsoft Access...	Displays the copyright notice, the software version number, and system information about your computer

DATABASE WINDOW MENU GUIDE

File Menu

New Database...   Creates a new, empty database. You specify the name of the database file and its location.

Open Database...   Retrieves an existing database from disk

Close Database...   Closes the open database file

New   Displays the New submenu

Table	Displays dialog box you use to begin construction of a new table
Query	Displays dialog box you use to begin construction of a new query
Form	Displays dialog box you use to begin construction of a new form
Report	Displays dialog box you use to begin construction of a new report
Macro	Displays dialog box you use to begin construction of a new macro
Module	Displays dialog box you use to begin construction of a new module

Rename...   Changes name of the selected database object

Output To...   Outputs the selected object to a file—probably so that the object's data can be used by another application

Import...   Creates an Access table and fills it with data from an external data source. You might use this command to permanently move tables from another database application to Microsoft Access.

Export...	Exports a Microsoft Access object—for example, a table. You might use this command to move tables from Access to another database application.
Attach Table...	Connects an external data source to an Access database so that you can query the data source from inside Access
Imp/Exp **S**etup...	Describes the way importing and exporting should work
P**r**int Setup...	Describes which printer Windows uses and how it should work
Print Pre<u>v</u>iew	Displays a window that shows how printed database objects look
Print...	Prints the open database object
Print De<u>f</u>inition...	Prints a description of the selected object's design
Sen**d**...	Sends the selected object's data in an electronic mail message
R**u**n Macro...	Starts a macro program
Add-<u>i</u>ns	Displays the Add-ins submenu
Add-in Manager	Adds and removes Add-in utilities such as the Query Wizards and the Form and Report Wizards
Database Documentor	Produces reports that describe database objects
Attachment Manager	Specifies which attached tables should be updated
Imp**o**rt Database...	Lets you import a database created by another database application
Menu Builder	Lets you build and modify custom menus
E**x**it	Closes, or stops, the Access application

Edit Menu Commands

Undo	Reverses, or undoes, the last database object change
Cut	Moves the current selection to the Clipboard
Copy	Moves a copy of the current selection to the Clipboard
Paste	Moves the Clipboard contents to the active database or object
D**e**lete	Erases the current selection
Relationships	Lets you view and edit relationships between tables and queries

View Menu Commands

Tables	Lists the table objects in the database
Queries	Lists the query objects in the database
Form	Lists the form objects in the database
Reports	Lists the report objects in the database
Macros	Lists the macro objects in the database
Modules	Lists the module objects in the database
Code...	Displays the Module window so that you can sling some code
Toolbars...	Specifies which toolbars show and how they look
Options...	Changes the way Access works and the way its windows look

Security Menu Commands

Permissions...	Specifies who can do what with database objects
Users...	Specifies who can and can't be members of the group that can use database objects
Groups...	Establishes a database user group
Change Password...	Specifies the password that provides access to a database
Change Owner...	Specifies which user owns, or controls, a database
Print Security...	Prints a bunch of information about groups and users

Window Menu

Tile	Arranges the open windows in a manner similar to the way ceramic tiles get arranged in a shower or a bath
Cascade	Arranges the open windows in a stack, but so that each window's title bar is visible
Arrange Icons	Arranges the minimized window icons into neat little rows
Hide	Removes the active object window from the Access application window
Unhide	Adds a previously hidden object window to the Access application window

About the numbered Window menu commands

The Window menu also lists as numbered commands the database window and any object windows. You can open a listed window by choosing the numbered command.

Help Menu

Contents	Lists the major Help topic categories
Search...	Provides help on a topic you specify
Cue Cards	Turns on Microsoft Access Cue Cards, which coach you through the steps for database management tasks
Technical Support...	Tells about support available for Access
About Microsoft Access...	Displays the copyright notice, the software version number, and system information about your computer

STANDARD TOOLBAR BUTTONS

Creates a new database file

Displays the Open Database dialog box so that you can retrieve an existing database

Connects an external data source's table to the open database

Prints the active database object

Shows what the printed pages of a database object will look like

Opens a window you use to write Access Basic code

Moves the current selection to the Clipboard

Moves a copy of the current selection to the Clipboard

Moves the Clipboard contents to the active database or object

Specifies table relationships

Imports database objects (such as tables) into Access

Exports database objects (such as tables) from Access

continues

Standard Toolbar Buttons *(continued)*

Exports table data to Microsoft Word so that data can be used in a mail merge

Exports a database object to Microsoft Excel

Creates a new query

Creates a new form

Creates a new report

Activates the database window

Automatically creates a form for the selected table or query

Automatically creates a report for the selected table or query

Undoes the last editing change

Tells Access to display those Cue Cards

Displays Help information about whatever you next click: a command, a piece of an object, or some element of the application or object window. Very handy.

E

F

G

H

I

J

U

The manuscript for this book was prepared and submitted to Microsoft Press in electronic form. Text files were prepared using Microsoft Word 2.0 for Windows. Pages were composed by Stephen L. Nelson, Inc., using PageMaker 5.0 for Windows, with text in Minion and display type in Copperplate. Composed pages were delivered to the printer as electronic prepress files.

COVER DESIGNER
Rebecca Geisler

COVER ILLUSTRATOR
Eldon Doty

INTERIOR TEXT DESIGNER
The Understanding Business

PAGE LAYOUT AND TYPOGRAPHY
Greg Schultz and Stefan Knorr

EDITOR
Pat Coleman

TECHNICAL EDITOR
Clay Martin

INDEXER
Julie Kawabata

Printed on recycled paper stock.

TRAIN YOURSELF
WITH *STEP BY STEP* BOOKS
FROM MICROSOFT PRESS

The *Step by Step* books are the perfect self-paced training solution for the businessperson. Whether you are a new user or are upgrading from a previous version of the software, the *Step by Step* books can teach you exactly what you need to know to get the most from your new software. Each lesson is modular, example-rich, and fully integrated with a timesaving practice file on the disk. So if you're too busy to attend class, or if classroom training doesn't make sense for you or your office, you can build the computer skills you need with the *Step by Step* books from Microsoft Press.

Microsoft Access® 2 for Windows™ Step by Step
Catapult, Inc.
375 pages, softcover with one 3.5-inch disk
$29.95 ($39.95 Canada)   ISBN 1-55615-593-X

Microsoft® Word 6 for Windows™ Step by Step
Catapult, Inc.
336 pages, softcover with one 3.5-inch disk
$29.95 ($39.95 Canada)   ISBN 1-55615-576-X

*Microsoft*Press